SIGNS OF THE HOLY ONE

UWE MICHAEL LANG

Signs of the Holy One

Liturgy, Ritual, and the Expression of the Sacred

IGNATIUS PRESS SAN FRANCISCO

Scripture quotations are from Revised Standard Version of the Bible—Second Catholic Edition © 2006 by the National Council of the Churches of Christ in the United States of America. All rights reserved.

Unless otherwise indicated, citations from papal documents, homilies, and interviews are largely taken from the Vatican website or www.news.va

Cover photograph:
Easter Vigil 2014 at the London Oratory
by Charles Cole

Cover design by Roxanne Mei Lum

ISBN 978-1-62164-007-3
Library of Congress Control Number 2014949952
Printed in the United States of America ♾

Contents

Acknowledgments

The ideas and arguments of this book have been presented at various conferences and seminars, and I am grateful to the audiences for the comment and criticism provided at these occasions. Some of the material has been published in an earlier form. Sections from chapters 2 and 3 are contained in "Sacred Architecture at the Service of the Mission of the Church", in *The Sacred Liturgy: Source and Summit of the Life and Mission of the Church: The Proceedings of the International Conference on the Sacred Liturgy*, ed. A. Reid, Sacra Liturgia 2013 (San Francisco: Ignatius Press, 2014), 187–211. Chapter 4 is a reworked version of "The Crisis of Sacred Art and the Sources for Its Renewal in the Thought of Pope Benedict XVI", in *Benedict XVI and the Sacred Liturgy: Proceedings of the First Fota International Liturgical Conference, 2008*, ed. N.J. Roy and J.E. Rutherford, Fota Liturgy Series (Dublin: Four Courts Press, 2010), 98–115. Chapter 5 makes use of "Theological Criteria for Sacred Music: From John XXII to Benedict XIV", in *Benedict XVI and Beauty in Sacred Music: Proceedings of the Third Fota International Liturgical Conference, 2010*, ed. J.E. Rutherford, Fota Liturgy Series, (Dublin and New York: Four Courts Press and Scepter Publishers, 2012), 41–59.

The writings on the liturgy by Joseph Ratzinger (Benedict XVI) are cited according to the recently published vol. 11 of *Joseph Ratzinger Collected Works: Theology of the Liturgy: The*

Sacramental Foundation of Christian Existence, ed. M. J. Miller, trans. J. Saward, K. Baker, S.J., H. Taylor et al. (San Francisco: Ignatius Press, 2014) [= JRCW 11].

I gratefully acknowledge my debt to those who have contributed to the actual writing of this book with their encouragement and critical feedback, Martin Mosebach, Matthew Levering, and especially Michael P. Foley, who read the entire manuscript and offered invaluable suggestions to improve its content and style. Thanks are due to Duncan Stroik and the Institute for Sacred Architecture in Notre Dame, Indiana, for making available the illustrations used in chapter 3, and to Charles Cole for allowing me to use his photo of the Easter Vigil 2014 at the London Oratory on the cover of this book.

Introduction

This book is the fruit of reflection on two sets of questions, which I consider essential for understanding the liturgy of the Western (Latin) Church, above all the Roman Rite, and its predicament in the contemporary world. The first set of questions emerges from the observation that the Church's solemn public worship speaks through a variety of "languages" other than language in the literal sense. These languages correspond to what the English social anthropologist Mary Douglas has described as "non-verbal symbols", which "are capable of creating a structure of meanings in which individuals can relate to one another and realize their own ultimate purposes".[1] The years when I was working for the Congregation for Divine Worship and the Discipline of the Sacraments in Rome (2008–2012) have sharpened my awareness of how important these non-linguistic or symbolic expressions are for the celebration of the Paschal Mystery, and I am convinced that they are more significant than language itself.

This would seem evident in today's world, which is dominated by images: on television, on computer screens, and on

[1] M. Douglas, *Natural Symbols: Explorations in Cosmology*, 2nd ed. (London and New York: Routledge, 1996), 53. While describing this cosmos of symbols as a "language" with "grammatical" rules and a specific "vocabulary", I do not commit myself to a structuralist model. On the usefulness and limits of "linguistic" approaches to the liturgy, see V. Turner, "Ritual, Tribal and Catholic", *Worship* 50 (1976): 504–26, at 510.

the ubiquitous mobile devices. We need to take account of the fact that we live in a "culture of images", as Joseph Cardinal Ratzinger wrote in his introduction to the *Compendium* of the *Catechism of the Catholic Church*, which he later approved as pope.[2] Today, the image tends to make a deeper and more lasting impression on people than the spoken word.

The power of the image has long been known in the Church's liturgical tradition, which has used sacred art and architecture as a medium of expression and communication. This has been noted by the (Lutheran) liturgical scholar Frank Senn in his enlightened discussion of the laity's participation in worship during the Middle Ages.[3] In more recent times Senn observes a tendency to see "liturgy only as text" and to limit participation in it to "speaking roles".[4] Affected by this tendency in the modern age, a broad stream

[2] J. Ratzinger, Introduction, *Compendium: Catechism of the Catholic Church* (Washington, D.C.: United States Conference of Catholic Bishops, 2006), xvii.

[3] "The laity have always found ways to participate in the liturgy, whether it was in their language or not, and they have always derived meaning from the liturgy, whether it was the intended meaning or not. Furthermore, the laity in worship were surrounded by other 'vernaculars' than language, not least of which were the church buildings themselves and the liturgical art that decorated them": F. C. Senn, *The People's Work: A Social History of the Liturgy* (Minneapolis: Fortress Press, 2006), 145.

[4] Ibid. A. Kavanagh, *On Liturgical Theology: The Hale Memorial Lectures of Seabury-Western Theological Seminary, 1981* (Collegeville, Minn.: Liturgical Press, 1984), 103–7, traces the reduction of liturgy to *text* to the Renaissance and Reformation periods and connects it with the invention of printing. "A Presence which had formerly been experienced by most as a kind of enfolding embrace had now modulated into an abecedarian printout to which only the skill of literacy could give complete access. . . . The truth lies now exclusively in the text; no longer on the wall, or in the windows, or in the liturgical activity of those who occupy the churches" (104). On the detrimental effect of printing on ritual, see also J. Bossy, *Christianity in the West, 1400–1700* (Oxford: Oxford University Press, 1985), 103.

of liturgical scholarship has focused on texts that are contained in written sources from late antiquity and the early Middle Ages, above all the oldest available sacramentaries. This approach is legitimate, at least to some extent, because the Church's public worship is ordered by the official texts she uses for it. Moreover, documents of the early liturgy are few, and the texts that have come down to us are our primary witnesses. However, even in the best scholarship of the last century, including that of Josef Andreas Jungmann, author of the magisterial work *Missarum sollemnia* on the Mass of the Roman Rite, it seems sometimes forgotten that the liturgy is not simply "a series of texts to be read, but rather a series of sacred actions to be done", as the musicologist and musician William P. Mahrt writes. "The solemn Mass consists of an integrated complex of words, music, and movement, together with other visual and even olfactory elements."[5] Mahrt published this analysis in 1975; since then progress has been made in the field, and scholars have taken note of the wider perspective of liturgical "vernaculars" evoked by Senn, which spoke so eloquently to worshippers in ages past.[6]

[5] W. P. Mahrt, "The Paradigm: The Musical Shape of the Liturgy, Part I: The Gregorian Mass in General", in Mahrt, *The Musical Shape of the Liturgy* (Richmond, Va.: Church Music Association of America, 2012), 3–16 (originally published 1975), at 5.

[6] J. F. Baldovin, *The Urban Character of Christian Worship: The Origins, Development, and Meaning of Stational Liturgy*, Orientalia Cristiana Analecta 228 (Rome: Pont. Institutum Studiorum Orientalium, 1987; anastatic reproduction 2002), 35, notes: "Historical understanding of Christian worship cannot rely on the texts of the liturgy alone. . . . Liturgy is a religious form, but it is also cultural, and as cultural it is subject to the vicissitudes of history. In other words, *context* is as . . . important as text for the history of worship." See also the work of E. Palazzo, "Art, Liturgy and the Five Senses in the Early Middle Ages", *Viator* 41 (2010): 25–56; "Art et liturgie au Moyen Âge: Nouvelles

The tendency to see liturgy primarily as text can also be observed on the official level: much of the reform of the Roman liturgy since the Second Vatican Council has been concerned with producing revised or new texts with insufficient regard for the complexity of ritual. In fact, leading exponents of social anthropology and ritual studies, above all Victor Turner, whose contributions will be discussed in the first chapter, have been critical of the postconciliar reform because of an apparent insensitivity to nonverbal signals and their meaning. Mary Douglas, a professed Catholic like Turner, wrote in the aftermath of the Council: "This is central to the difficulties of Christianity today. It is as if the liturgical signal boxes were manned by colour-blind signalmen."[7] It was the merit of James Hitchcock's *The Recovery of the Sacred* (1974) to show to a broader audience the significance of ritual studies for understanding the liturgy and for evaluating the contemporary efforts of its renewal. David Torevell has taken up this approach in a more systematic manner in his *Losing the Sacred: Ritual, Modernity and Liturgical Reform* (2000).[8]

---

approches anthropologique et épistémologique", in *Anales de Historia del Arte*, Volumen extraordinario 2010: 31–74; "La dimension sonore de la liturgie dans l'Antiquité chrétienne et au Moyen Âge", in *Archéologie du son: Les dispositifs de pots acoustiques dans les édifices anciens*, ed. B. Palazzo-Bertholon and J.-C. Valière, Supplément au Bulletin monumental 5 (Paris: Société Française d'Archéologie, 2012), 51–58.

[7] Douglas, *Natural Symbols*, 44; cf. xii, 1 and 53. See also the provocative book of A. Archer, *The Two Catholic Churches: A Study in Oppression* (London: SCM Press, 1986), chap. 7: "Vatican II and the Passing of the Simple Faithful", 126–46.

[8] J. Hitchcock, *The Recovery of the Sacred* (New York: Seabury Press, 1974), and D. Torevell, *Losing the Sacred: Ritual, Modernity and Liturgical Reform* (Edinburgh: T&T Clark, 2000).

The Holy See has been mainly occupied with the *recognitio* of liturgical texts and translations. This is necessary and important, and some sterling work has been produced in recent years, especially the revision of the postconciliar translation of the *Missale Romanum*, most notably in the English language.[9] However, such legitimate emphasis tends to underestimate the fact that the *lex orandi* expressing the *lex credendi* is much more than just text: it includes gestures and postures, movements and processions, music, architecture, art, and so on. An example of this tendency would be the 1970 *editio typica* of the *Missale Romanum* of Pope Paul VI. Unlike preceding editions of the Missal going back to the medieval manuscript tradition, the book contains only the liturgical texts, with no musical notation at all.[10] This lacuna has been addressed to some degree in the third *editio typica* of 2002, which has many texts in musical notation, but still not the Prefaces that form part of the *Ordo Missae*. Hence a solemn celebration of the Ordinary Form of the Roman Rite in Latin on a "green" Sunday in the liturgical year still needs to resort to other books, such as the Solesmes version of the *Ordo Missae in cantu*.[11] The institution of a new office within the Congregation for Divine Worship and the

[9] I have discussed the importance of liturgical language in *The Voice of the Church at Prayer: Reflections on Liturgy and Language* (San Francisco: Ignatius Press, 2012).

[10] *Missale Romanum ex decreto Sacrosancti Oecumenici Concilii Vaticani II instauratum auctoritate Pauli PP. VI promulgatum*. Editio typica (Vatican City: Typis Polyglottis Vaticanis, 1970).

[11] *Missale Romanum ex decreto Sacrosancti Oecumenici Concilii Vaticani II instauratum auctoritate Pauli PP. VI promulgatum Ioannis Pauli PP. II cura recognitum*. Editio typica tertia, reimpressio emendata (Vatican City: Typis Vaticanis, 2008). *Ordo Missae in cantu iuxta editionem typicam tertiam Missalis Romani* (Solesmes: Éd. de Solesmes, 2012).

Discipline of the Sacraments on November 14, 2012, dedicated to liturgical music and art, is a sign of hope that more attention will be given to these essential aspects of the Church's *lex orandi.*

The second set of questions emerges from my work in the subject areas of sacred music, art, and architecture. During my years in Rome I taught for (and for three years directed) the master's degree course in Architecture, Sacred Arts, and Liturgy at the Università Europea di Roma. Initially, this work focused on the concept of beauty and its theological dimension. However, the problem became more and more evident to me that, in the context of modernity, one can reason about beauty only to a very limited extent. Beauty has been reduced to a subjective judgment, and, for those who do not share the presuppositions of the classical philosophical tradition, it remains an elusive concept. When it comes to church architecture, for instance, recourse to beauty will not carry us very far. We may not think that Renzo Piano's church of Saint Pius of Pietrelcina in San Giovanni Rotondo works *as* a church, but how do we respond to someone who finds its architectural forms, or the space it creates for the assembly, "beautiful"?

For these reasons I propose that any discussion of sacred architecture, art, and music needs to be clear about what is meant by the attribute "sacred". Social anthropology and ritual studies have dedicated much attention to the question of the sacred, and it will be useful to give an overview of this complex and diverse conversation (chapter 1).

While the category of the sacred often seems to be taken for granted, its significance for Christianity has been contested or even rejected. Hence its theological foundations need to be revisited and, where necessary, reconstructed. The task is not straightforward and must include an evaluation of Karl Rahner's contribution to the subject. At its conclusion, however, we arrive at a more mature understanding of what makes the liturgy sacred (chapter 2).

The following chapter explores how this renewed conception of the sacred can be translated into the design of churches. Particular attention will be given to questions raised by contemporary church building. The chapter ends with a proposal of theological principles to be observed in sacred architecture (chapter 3).

The search for beauty is resumed in the chapter on sacred art. The difficulty of this search in the philosophical context of modernity is felt very clearly. In the face of this aporia, I shall attempt to sketch the elements of a theological response on the foundation of the Second Vatican Council's Constitution on the Sacred Liturgy and other documents of the Church's Magisterium (chapter 4).

While the title of the following chapter, "Between Theological Millstones" may appear overly dramatic, I contend that it adequately characterizes the situation of church music today. The intimate relationship of sacred music with divine worship makes it particularly susceptible to tendentious theological impositions and sensitive to questionable cultural incretions. A brief historical overview will show that the contemporary problems concerning sacred music are not new and will help to find ways toward a genuine renewal (chapter 5).

In this book I often engage with the thought of Joseph Ratzinger (Benedict XVI), both his writings as a theologian and his teachings as pope. The depth and breadth of these contributions make them indispensable for the ongoing conversation about the sacred liturgy and its related fields.

I

Ritual and the Sacred: Anthropological Foundations

Before looking at the sacred from a theological and liturgical perspective, I propose to consider what social anthropology and ritual studies have to say on the subject. There are properly theological reasons for choosing this approach. Following Thomas Aquinas' adage that "grace does not destroy nature but perfects it",[1] it is evident that any understanding of ritual and sacrality in Catholic worship will rely on foundations that can be described as common characteristics of world religions. As will be seen, the theological arguments build on and respond to theories of myth, ritual, and religion that have been discussed in the course of the last two centuries. The concerns of theologians can be illuminated against the background of this lively and intriguing field of research.

Moreover, in the contemporary situation the problems begin precisely at this point. Josef Pieper has observed that the process identified as "secularization" of the Western world is not simply a dechristianization; rather, we witness a progressive decline of *natural* religiosity. Ideas, attitudes, and practices that formed a shared heritage of many of the world's religious traditions have lost their hold on the modern mind. The Christian faith cannot do without such a sense of the

[1] "Gratia non tollit, sed perficit naturam". Thomas Aquinas, *Summa Theologiae* I, q. 1, a. 8 ad 2.

sacred, even if it significantly transforms and transcends it. If, then, this sensitivity is gradually weakened or even lost, there will be little for Christianity on which to build. In Pieper's own words, "the hand with which man is able to grasp what is authentically Christian threatens to wither."[2]

In order to understand how the *proprium Christianum* rests on this common foundation and, at the same time, distinguishes itself from it, this chapter will present essential contributions toward a study of ritual and the sacred. This is not an easy undertaking, because many complex and diverse theories have been proposed. As Catherine Bell notes, there is no simple evolution or advance in this field of research. Scholars use different methodologies that are sometimes complementary and sometimes in conflict with one another. Hardly any theory is completely original and autonomous; in fact, most of them build on earlier approaches or are formulated in opposition to them.[3] My own discussion will inevitably be eclectic, with the purpose of establishing tools for analysis.

[2] J. Pieper, "Zur Fernseh-Übertragung der Heiligen Messe (1953)", in Pieper, *Werke*, vol. 7: *Religionsphilosophische Schriften*, ed. B. Wald (Hamburg: Felix Meiner, 2000), 487–90, at 487: "Auf dem Grunde des geschichtlichen Vorgangs, den wir als 'Säkularisierung' bezeichnen, geschieht vor allem eine fortschreitende Schwächung der *natürlichen* religiösen Grundvorstellungen. Es handelt sich um etwas, das fast noch schlimmer und hoffnungsloser ist als 'Entchristlichung', weil sozusagen die Hand zu verdorren droht, mit welcher der Mensch das eigentlich Christliche zu fassen vermag. Weil aber andererseits der Vorgang nicht formell und unmittelbar 'Entchristlichung' ist, setzt er sich um so leichter und unmerklicher innerhalb der Christenheit selbst durch."

[3] C. Bell, *Ritual: Perspectives and Dimensions* (New York: Oxford University Press, 1997), 88–89; see also her *Ritual Theory, Ritual Practice* (New York: Oxford University Press, 1992, reprinted 2009).

The Sacred

The sociological approach to religion was shaped decisively by the work of Émile Durkheim, who sees religion as a social institution that establishes and maintains the workings of a society. In his classic work on *The Elementary Forms of the Religious Life* (*Les formes élémentaires de la vie religieuse*, published in 1912), Durkheim defines a religion as

> a unified system of beliefs and practices relative to sacred things, that is to say, things set apart and forbidden—beliefs and practices which unite into one single moral community called a Church, all those who adhere to them.[4]

The sacred is thus defined as that which is set apart and cannot be approached or accessed in any ordinary way. Note that Durkheim sees a categorical difference and radical heterogeneity between sacred and profane: "between the two there is no common measure".[5] The separation between the two spheres is effected by ritual; however, this is not the only function of rites: they also have an important effect on the community by establishing identity and solidarity among those who participate in them. Characteristically, Durkheim is interested in the social function of ritual, particularly in the way its participants are transformed and acquire a new status, which is most obvious in initiation rites.[6]

[4] É. Durkheim, *The Elementary Forms of the Religious Life*, trans. J. W. Swain (London: Allen & Unwin, 1915), 47. For a discussion of the historical, and in particular biographical, context of Durkheim's work, see G. Lynch, *On the Sacred* (Durham: Acumen, 2012), 15–38. Lynch sees his book as a contribution to maintain Durkheim's legacy.

[5] Ibid., 62.

[6] Cf. D. Torevell, *Losing the Sacred: Ritual, Modernity and Liturgical Reform* (Edinburgh: T&T Clark, 2000), 1–5.

Durkheim's theory was criticized early on both for the dubious empirical data on which it relied and for its procrustean theory. What is significant for our study, however, is his conceptualization of sacred and profane, which has had a lasting influence. Durkheim speaks of an "abyss" that separates the two worlds,[7] and this idea has been taken up in different ways by Rudolf Otto and Mircea Eliade.

While Durkheim considered religion a social construct (albeit the most essential one) and had no regard for its spiritual or metaphysical dimensions, Otto, a Lutheran theologian, rejected such a reductionist approach and described the experience of "the holy" as a universal and irreducible phenomenon. In his work *The Idea of the Holy* (*Das Heilige*, published in 1917), Otto develops a phenomenology of religion centered on the experience of "the holy" (the original German expression also allows for the English rendering "the sacred") as something "wholly other". The awareness of the holy as the "numinous", a word coined by Otto after the Latin term *numen* for divine power, is explained as non-rational, non-sensory and transcending the subject; it inspires holy fear and awe (*mysterium tremendum*).[8] Otto's theory is often considered indebted to Friedrich Schleiermacher's understanding of religion as the feeling of "absolute dependence". However, he departed from what he saw as Schleiermacher's implicit naturalism, which would not account for the numinous as a presence outside of the self; hence he preferred the expression "creature-feeling (*Krea-*

[7] Durkheim, *Elementary Forms*, 61 and 318.

[8] R. Otto, *The Idea of the Holy: An Inquiry into the Non-Rational Factor in the Idea of the Divine and Its Relation to the Rational*, trans. J. W. Harvey, revised with additions (Oxford and London: Oxford University Press and Humphrey Milford, 1936).

turgefühl)", which has a transcendent connotation.[9] Otto focused on the individual and was concerned above all with the mystical experience of the holy not only in Christianity but also in other religions. While his seminal work has an appendix with a section on "The Numinous in Hymn and Liturgy",[10] he does not seem to be interested in ritual as such (as would be typical of a German Lutheran scholar of his generation).

Similar to Otto in his phenomenological and anti-reductionist approach to religion, Eliade proposed a clear separation between sacred and profane. He defines the sacred as "the opposite of the profane" and as "the manifestation of something of a wholly different order" from ordinary reality. This manifestation of the sacred, the "wholly other", he calls "hierophany".[11] Eliade evokes Durkheim's "abyss that divides the two modalities of experience"[12] and in the course of his work analyzes how the *homo religiosus* of traditional societies experiences the sacred in space, time, nature, and self as a reality that establishes order in the world. Eliade's theory gives primacy to myth and symbols and relegates ritual to a secondary level. In Bell's reading of Eliade, "myth and symbols provide a clearer and more spontaneous view of the various forms in which humans experience and express the sacred than is afforded by ritual". Myth expresses "beliefs, symbols, and ideas" as a primary manifestation of the sacred, whereas ritual is considered "a reenactment of

[9] Cf. A. Dole, "Schleiermacher and Otto on Religion", *Religious Studies* 40 (2004): 389–413.

[10] Otto, *Idea of the Holy*, 193–94.

[11] M. Eliade, *The Sacred and the Profane: The Nature of Religion*, trans. W.R. Trask (New York: Harcourt Brace, 1959), 10 and 11.

[12] Ibid., 14.

a cosmogonic event or story recounted in myth'', such as new year rituals of cosmic regeneration, and hence are a secondary expression of it.[13]

The importance of ritual in relation to the sacred was recognized by Arnold van Gennep, a critic of Durkheim and known for his work *The Rites of Passage* (*Les rites de passage*, published in 1909), in which he studied the rites that mark an individual's change of status in social life. Van Gennep identified a sequence of three stages in such rites of passage: separation, transition (or liminality), and incorporation.[14] This scheme works particularly well with initiation rites, but is also applied to marriages and funerals. Van Gennep's functionalist method provides an important supplement and, in some ways, correction to Durkheim's and Eliade's analysis of the sacred as a kind of absolute reality that manifests itself spontaneously in the world. According to Bell, van Gennep considered the sacred a relative entity or quality ''that readily shifts in different situations and at different ritual stages''. By speaking about the ''pivoting of the sacred'', Van Gennep highlighted ritual's active role in defining what is sacred; it does ''not simply react to the sacred as something already and for always fixed''.[15]

Ritual

Ritual is about symbolic performance and communication. It generally consists of prescribed actions that are carried out in a deliberate and stylized manner; its use of language is

[13] Bell, *Ritual*, 10–11.

[14] See A. Van Gennep, *The Rites of Passage*, trans. M. B. Vizedom and G. L. Caffee (Chicago: University of Chicago Press, 1960), 3.

[15] Bell, *Ritual*, 37, with reference to Gennep, *Rites of Passage*, 12.

highly formalized. The best definition of ritual I have found is that of Stanley J. Tambiah:

> Ritual is a culturally constructed system of symbolic communication. It is constituted of patterned and ordered sequences of words and acts, often expressed in multiple media, whose content and arrangement are characterised in varying degree by formality (conventionality), stereotypy (rigidity), condensation (fusion), and redundancy (repetition).[16]

As a highly structured and ordered system of communication, ritual is often compared with play. However, Tambiah insists that there is an important difference between them: games "appear to have a disjunctive effect: they end in the establishment of a difference between the individual players or teams where originally there was no indication of inequality". Ritual, by contrast, has the effect of establishing or confirming solidarity or communion between separate groups.[17]

What both ritual and play have in common is the fact that the end or purpose of either lies in itself: thereby, it effects a change or transformation in those who participate in it. As such, ritual is efficacious and acts by means of symbols.[18] In a Christian context, the sacraments would be obvious examples of actions and words effecting a state that would not be present otherwise, for instance, in the symbolic act of pouring water three times over a person's head with

[16] S.J. Tambiah, "A Performative Approach to Ritual", *Proceedings of the British Academy* 65 (1979): 113–69, at 119.

[17] Ibid., 118.

[18] Cf. Torevell, *Losing the Sacred*, 36, with reference to the work of Richard Schechner.

the formula "I baptize you in the name of the Father and of the Son and of the Holy Spirit."

While ritual behavior is part of our daily lives and is not limited to religion, it is here where it is most widely perceived and practiced. In his highly influential work on the interpretation of cultures, Clifford Geertz describes religion as a

> (1) system of symbols which acts to (2) establish powerful, pervasive, and long-lasting moods and motivations in men by (3) formulating conceptions of a general order of existence and (4) clothing these conceptions which such an aura of factuality that (5) the moods and motivations seem uniquely realistic.[19]

This dense description hinges on Geertz's understanding of "symbol", for which he proposes a broad definition. The term is used for "any object, act, event, quality, or relation which serves as a vehicle for a conception". The conception is the symbol's "meaning": thus the Cross, when spoken about, represented visually, or formed as a physical gesture, is a symbol. Geertz further describes symbols as "tangible formulations of notions, abstractions from experience fixed in perceptible forms, concrete embodiments of ideas, attitudes, judgments, longings, or beliefs".[20] By means of such symbols, a religion shapes and directs the dispositions, attitudes, ideas, and incentives of its adherents. As a system of symbols, religion articulates and communicates conceptions about the whole cosmos. In doing so, it proposes a model *of* reality as well as a model *for* reality, that is, it claims to represent things as they are and to show how they should be.

[19] C. Geertz, "Religion as a Cultural System", in Geertz, *The Interpretation of Cultures: Selected Essays* (New York: Basic Books, 1973), 87–125, at 90.
[20] Ibid., 91.

In other words, religion provides a world view and creates an ethos.

For Geertz, religion as a system of symbols does not simply reflect social structure (in a Durkheimian way); however, it is not totally independent of it, either. The symbolism relates to such human experiences as ignorance, pain, and injustice and gives them meaning by integrating them into a cosmic order. In ritual, this general order of existence (the world as it is) and the ethos (the world as it should be and what we should do about it) meet. The complex of symbols imbues "the metaphysic they formulate and the style of life they recommend" with "persuasive authority". In fact, Geertz even speaks of a fusion of the two in ritual: "The world as lived and the world as imagined, fused under the agency of a single set of symbolic forms, turn out to be the same world." Religious convictions emerge from such "concrete acts of religious observance".[21] Geertz would seem to reformulate the Christian principle *lex orandi, lex credendi*: the liturgy is an expression of and witness to belief.[22] There is, however, a significant difference here for which Geertz would not seem to account. As Aidan Kavanagh observes, in the Christian understanding, rite "forms and constitutes but does not 'produce' the *lex credendi*".[23]

[21] Ibid., 112–13.

[22] The principle "ut legem credendi lex statuat supplicandi" was first formulated by Prosper of Aquitaine in the fifth century; see H. Denzinger, *Enchiridion Symbolorum: Compendium of Creeds, Definitions, and Declarations of the Catholic Church*, ed. P. Hünermann, H. Hoping, R. Fastiggi, and A. Englund Nash, 43rd ed. (San Francisco: Ignatius Press, 2012), no. 246.

[23] A. Kavanagh, *On Liturgical Theology: The Hale Memorial Lectures of Seabury-Western Theological Seminary, 1981* (Collegeville, Minn.: Liturgical Press, 1984), 100.

How Does Ritual "Work"?

Granted that we accept this understanding of ritual, we may ask whether ritual is always successful in doing what it is meant to do. In other words, what does it take for ritual to "work"? A step toward answering this question is made by Roy Rappaport's distinction between "indexical" and "canonical" messages in ritual.[24] In all rituals, participants transmit indexical or self-referential messages about their current states, which can be physical, psychological, or social. However, in some, though not all, rituals, the participants also transmit canonical messages about "enduring aspects of nature, society, or cosmos". These messages are not variable but stable and are transmitted by the formal and symbolical elements of the ritual.[25] Rappaport adduces the example of the Roman liturgy: the Order of Mass, he notes, "does not, in itself, express anything about the current states of those performing it".[26] In fact, the canonical aspect in the Mass is so dominant that the indexical aspect appears trivial. And yet, Rappaport argues,

> in all religious rituals, there is transmitted an indexical message that cannot be transmitted in any other way and, far from being trivial, it is one without which canonical messages are without force, or may even seem nonsensical.[27]

A "working" ritual would appear to depend on the integration of canonical and indexical messages. To take the example of the penitential rite: the confession of sins, with its

[24] R. A. Rappaport, *Ecology, Meaning, and Religion* (Richmond, Calif.: North Atlantic Books, 1979), 179–82.

[25] Ibid., 182.

[26] Ibid., 179.

[27] Ibid., 182.

ritual expression of bowing down and beating one's breast, is a canonical element of the Mass. At the same time, the participants must be able to make this confession their own and hence turn it into an indexical message. If this does not happen, the ritual is emptied of its meaning. The complex of ritual gestures in the liturgy of the Mass, such as standing, kneeling, making the sign of the cross, and so on, are canonical messages that are meant to be appropriated by the worshippers as indexical.

In liturgical celebrations it is not only the stable parts, such as the Order of Mass and the Rites of Baptism and of the other sacraments, that communicate canonical messages. The variable parts, which change with the seasons and feasts of the liturgical year, likewise do not necessarily tell us about the present states of those involved in them. Rather, they aim at expressing the thoughts, feelings, and aspirations of the participants in such a way that the canonical and the indexical aspects of the rite merge. In other words, the liturgy prompts the faithful to insert themselves into the mystery of faith that is being celebrated. For instance, the liturgy of Christmas Day, through its prayers, readings, and chants, is meant to arouse among the people joy and wonder at the birth of the Savior in Bethlehem. Or to cite another example that strikes a chord with many Catholics (and not only those) even today: the sober liturgy of Ash Wednesday, with the blessing and imposition of ashes, is meant to evoke a sense of conversion and penance. Where such sentiments and thoughts are genuine, an integration if not fusion of canonical and indexical messages has been achieved.

Rappaport's distinction between indexical and canonical messages also provides a hermeneutical tool for understanding movements of reform and renewal of the liturgy in the Catholic Church. When the integration of canonical and indexical messages is no longer successful (or at least no longer perceived as such), there will be pressure for ritual change, and such pressure has now driven the history of the Roman liturgy for more than a century. However, the question of ritual change is a delicate one and has been described by social anthropologists as a problem in itself. This is so because rituals present themselves "as the unchanging, time-honored customs of an enduring community", and they derive their legitimacy from age and tradition.[28] It is the stability that makes the rite, even when it allows for carefully integrated exceptions. Changes in ritual, especially when they are introduced in an abrupt way, impair the meaning of received symbols and convey the message that their observance was not so important after all. Even more, they can lead to an alienation from symbolism as such by suggesting its irrelevance.[29]

This can be illustrated with an example from the liturgical reform following the Second Vatican Council: the removal of the Eucharistic tabernacle from its central position at the high altar of the church to a peripheral place in the sanctuary or even to a side chapel. From a historical perspective, the fixed high-altar tabernacle is a relatively recent introduction: it emerged in the Italian Renaissance along with a type of church building that discarded the medieval system of partitions in order to create a unified interior space. This idea was promoted in the Catholic Reform of the sixteenth century, and so the tabernacle placed at the high altar became the focal point of Baroque sacred architecture (and of popular piety).[30] It is a well-known fact that there had been various

[28] Bell, *Ritual*, 210.

[29] Cf. J. Hitchcock, *The Recovery of the Sacred* (New York: Seabury Press, 1974), 77–79 and 130–37.

[30] A brief overview of this development can be found in U.M. Lang,

forms of Eucharistic reservation before, and some of these forms were restored in the postconciliar period. A merely historical perspective, however, falls short of the symbolic dimension of such a change in its given context. The high-altar tabernacle presented itself as the immemorial custom of Western Catholicism. By moving the reserved Eucharist to a less prominent place in the church building, the message was conveyed that it had become less important for the worship and life of the people. The impression was given that the reserved Sacrament was "dethroned",[31] in particular where it was replaced by the priest's chair (in imitation of the bishop's seat in ancient Roman basilicas). Whatever the particular merits of this shift may be, a stable existing custom cannot simply be substituted without a loss of symbolic meaning.

The Work of Victor Turner

Victor Turner, a noted anthropologist and committed Catholic, has not only made significant contributions to ritual studies but also engaged with liturgical scholarship. In particular, Turner saw in the traditional forms of the Roman Rite, with its various genres of nonverbal, sensory elements,

"Tamquam Cor in Pectore: The Eucharistic Tabernacle before and after the Council of Trent", *Sacred Architecture Journal* 15 (2009): 32–34. For a positive evaluation of the Baroque conception of liturgical space as *teatro sacro* (sacred theatre), see now R. van Bühren, "Kirchenbau in Renaissance und Barock: Liturgiereformen und ihre folgen für Raumordnung, liturgische Disposition und Bildausstattung nach dem Trienter Konzil", in *Operation am lebenden Objekt: Roms Liturgiereformen von Trient bis zum Vaticanum II*, ed. S. Heid (Berlin: be.bra wissenschaft, 2014), 93–119.

[31] Cf. Hitchcock, *Recovery of the Sacred*, 168.

an example of what he calls "living" or "authentic" ritual. In it

> what is usually left implicit, or even suppressed, in the flow of ordinary social life, is revealed; the deepest meaning people have come to assign to key features of personal and social experience. Living ritual captures and preserves these meanings in symbolic form, elaborated into patterns which please as well as edify.[32]

Living ritual, thus conceived, achieves what Rappaport terms a successful integration of indexical and canonical messages. For Turner, such integration is

> the reflexive outcome of the passionate thought and experiential wisdom of many together through many generations of shared and directly transmitted social life. It is therefore directed to the constancies of the human condition, to which it applies the teaching and example of its religious founders and teachers. Embedded in its structure are remedies for ills as well as signposts to salvation from the turbulence of disorderly purposes.[33]

This description approaches a theological definition of rite as "a living form of *paradosis*, the handing-on of tradition", as formulated by Joseph Ratzinger.[34]

[32] V. Turner, "Ritual, Tribal and Catholic", *Worship* 50 (1976): 504–26, at 506–7.

[33] Ibid., 507.

[34] "The 'rite', that form of celebration and prayer which has ripened in the faith and the life of the Church, is a condensed form of living tradition (. . .) and thus at the same time the fellowship of generations one with another becomes something we can experience, fellowship with the people who pray before us and after us. Thus the rite is something of benefit which is given to the Church, a living form of *paradosis*, the handing-on of tradition": J. Ratzinger, preface to *The Organic Development of the Liturgy: The Principles of Liturgical Reform and Their Relation to the Twentieth-Century Liturgical Movement Prior to the Second Vatican Council*, by A. Reid, 2nd ed. (San Francisco: Ignatius Press, 2005), 9–13, at 11 (JRCW 11:591).

Turner calls this successful integration, in which the participants in a ritual place "their current lives in vital relation to a supremely noble paradigm", an "exalted state of reflexivity".[35] Furthermore, he describes the conditions for making this state possible as "flow" and "frame".[36] On this account, flow is

> a state in which action follows action according to an internal logic which seems to need no conscious intervention on our part; we experience it as a unified flowing from one moment to the next, in which we feel in control of our actions, and in which there is little distinction between self and environment, between stimulus and response, or between past, present and future.[37]

This common experience of "flow" is by no means restricted to religion but can be shared in play or sport or in the creations of music, art, and literature. Its paradigm, however, is sacred ritual. Turner identifies several elements constitutive of flow in ritual, which I shall present here in synthesis.[38]

Above all, flow is characterized by a merging of action and consciousness: actors in a successful ritual are not self-conscious of what they are doing; if they become so, the flow is interrupted and ease turns into anxiety. This lack of self-consciousness is made possible by a "limited stimulus field", the rules of which can be easily mastered. In a game, there are precise formal rules; in the liturgy there are rubrics.[39]

[35] Turner, "Ritual", 520.

[36] He does so with reference to the work of M. Csikszentmihalyi, *Beyond Boredom and Anxiety* (San Francisco: Jossey-Bass, 1975).

[37] Turner, "Ritual", 520.

[38] Ibid, 520–22.

[39] Cf. the observations of Kavanagh, *On Liturgical Theology*, 102: "Rite is sustained by rote and obedience far more than by restless creativity, and

Moreover, a ritual that flows gives clear instructions for action and unambiguous feedback to it. Such coherence is rarely present in ordinary activities.

Consequently, the actors sense themselves in control of their actions and of the environment because their skills are perfectly matched to the demands of the ritual; this is achieved thanks to the limited number of rules and to their mastery of them. Outside the particular context a rite or game provides, such a sense of control is difficult to attain owing to the enormous complexity of the world. Also, the self retreats, and deviant or eccentric behavior is reduced, when all actors who are immersed in the ritual accept its framing rules as binding.

Finally, flow has no end or purpose outside itself; it is "autotelic" and can be a source of happiness and even pleasure, which does not contradict the ascetic dimension it evidently requires. Where people do not have access to this experience in religious ritual (for whatever reason), it will be sought in other contexts, such as music, art, sport, or even a computer game. Turner describes such activity as characteristic of modern industrial society and as merely resembling liminality because of its optional and fragmentary character; he therefore calls it "liminoid".[40]

A ritual system also has its moments when the flow is deliberately halted or even contravened. Turner cites the exam-

---

obedience is a subordinate part of the larger virtue of justice while creativity is not. In our day it seems to require more courage to obey a rubric or law than to break it. Creativity of the Spontaneous Me variety condemns rite and symbol to lingering deaths by trivialization, bemusing those who would communicate by rite and symbol to a point where they finally wander away in search of something which appears to be more stable and power-laden."

[40] See V. Turner and E. Turner, *Image and Pilgrimage in Christian Culture: Anthropological Perspectives* (New York: Columbia University Press, 1978), 253.

ple of Good Friday in the liturgical year, when the church is stripped of its ornaments and when the customary celebration of the Mass is replaced with the austere liturgy of the Passion. Another example for such a deliberate interruption of the ritual flow would be the homily in the Mass after the proclamation of the Gospel (or, as in some medieval uses of the Roman Rite, after the Creed).

The Catholic liturgical tradition represents for Turner an eminent example of a complex ritual system, shaped and reshaped over many generations and yet, in its totality and integrity, not contingent upon these historical determinations. As a ritual system, it embodies "a deep knowledge of the nature of flow, and how and where to break it in order to instil truths about the nature of time, the human condition, and evil". The flow it creates is not just for individuals in their personal prayer or meditation but for the whole community at worship: it is a "shared flow".[41]

In parentheses, it may be added that Turner's description of "flow" in ritual explains a problem experienced today in the revival of the traditional Latin liturgy, now established as the "Extraordinary Form" of the Roman Rite. Celebrations of this form often do not flow precisely because the participants, both the officiating clergy and the participating laity, are too self-conscious of what they are doing. In the first instance, this may be for lack of familiarity with the rite itself: the clergy tend to think at every step about what to do next, while the laity find it difficult to follow, flicking through their missals or prayer books. Once the celebration has become more stable and regular, such difficulties subside and the rite can indeed "flow". This is beautifully seen, for instance, in Benedictine monasteries, such as Fontgombault,

[41] Cf. Turner, "Ritual", 523.

Le Barroux, or Norcia, where this rite is part of the monks' daily observance. However, there is another reason for this problem, which lies in the fact that the liturgy is celebrated as a rejection of something and hence is turned into a political statement (both in the ecclesiastical and in the secular sense). This reactionary stance militates against ritual flow because the motive for participating is not a "natural" attraction to the sacred but an "artificial" preoccupation with conflicts that are extrinsic to the liturgy at hand. In other words, ideological preoccupation complicates and even negates the indexical side of the ritual and can so block its flow.

Returning to Turner's analysis, it comes as no surprise that he was very critical of the reform of the Roman Rite that followed the Second Vatican Council. In fact, he saw more common elements between its preconciliar form and the wider religious traditions of humanity, such as the ritual system of the Ndembu of Zambia, which he studied extensively, than between either of them and the postconciliar liturgy. Admittedly, Turner witnessed the moment of the greatest liturgical upheaval and confusion in the Catholic Church. However, his critique should be heeded, because it does ask penetrating questions. When worship is meant to be reformed in order to be more "relevant" to "modern man"—as was an aim explicitly stated by so many protagonists of the liturgical reform[42]—it is *de facto* conceived in a Durkheimian manner as an expression or reflection of contemporary social structures. Once these structures change, as has happened in a drastic way in the modern age, espe-

[42] See the well-documented study of Reid, *Organic Development of the Liturgy*, chap. 3: "The Liturgical Movement and Liturgical Reform from 1948 to the Second Vatican Council", 145–301, esp. 214–19 on Annibale Bugnini.

cially since the Industrial Revolution, it is suggested that the liturgy needs to change, too.[43]

While there is indeed a correlation between religion as a system of symbols and social structures, it is a complex and subtle one, as Geertz shows. For Turner, it was a strength of the traditional Roman liturgy

> that it could be performed by the most diverse groups and individuals, surmounting their divisions of age, sex, ethnicity, culture, economic status or political affiliation. The liturgy stood out as a magnificent objective creation, a vehicle for every sort of Christian interiority, if the will to use it lovingly and well was there.[44]

Turner can of course be criticized for an ahistorical perspective on the Catholic liturgy, which is limited to the

[43] Turner sees this problem in *Sacrosanctum Concilium*: "The Constitution on the Sacred Liturgy was clearly influenced by structural-functionalism, which holds that ritual structure reflects social structure—hence should change in response to social structural changes—and that the 'social function' of ritual is to reanimate periodically the 'sentiments' on which a given social formation depends for its successful running. It was also influenced by behaviorism with its assumption that the faithful can be 'conditioned' by 'reinforcement' to accept what Establishment theoreticians of liturgy regard as being sociologically appropriate and hence 'good' for them. Both structural-functionalism and behaviorism are obsolete formulations since they depend upon the metaphor or model of society as a closely integrated system, like an organism or a machine, rather than upon regarding it as a process with some systematic characteristics, a process that moves necessarily through creative moments of anti-structure as well as through long periods of structural regularity"; V. Turner, "Passages, Margins, and Poverty: Religious Symbols of Communitas", *Worship* 46 (1972): 390–412 and 482–94, at 392.

[44] Turner, "Ritual", 525. Cf. the fascinating case study on the many ways in which people participated in the preconciliar liturgy by S. Gilley, "Roman Liturgy and Popular Piety: The 'Devotional Revolution' in Irish Catholicism", in *The Genius of the Roman Rite: Historical, Theological and Pastoral Perspectives on Catholic Liturgy. Proceedings of the 2006 Oxford CIEL Colloquium*, ed. U.M. Lang (Chicago: Hillenbrand Books, 2010), 216–34.

unusually stable period between the post-Tridentine revision and Vatican II. The history of the Roman Rite shows considerable diversity and discontinuity, and not a few of its elements actually owe their introduction to contemporary social structures, beginning with the signs of honor awarded to bishops when they were given the status of high officials of the Roman Empire (incense, candles, seat in the center of the apse of a basilica). Such legitimate criticism notwithstanding, the weight of Turner's analysis is shown not least in the fact that it was published in *Worship*, an American journal fully committed to the more radical expressions of liturgical reform. In these contributions, Turner expressed his fear "that the tendentious manipulation of particular interest groups, prestigiously and strategically situated in the Church, is liquidating the ritual bonds which held the entire heterogeneous mystical body together in worship".[45] While this appears to be a stark overstatement, there are symptoms in liturgical practice today that would vindicate Turner. These symptoms are not sufficiently understood if they are simply classified as liturgical abuses, that is, violations of liturgical law.[46] In a world of unprecedented mobility and globalization, the prevalence of particular interests often makes Catholic worship parochial and fragmented in ways that go far beyond the question of using the vernacular. It is properly the "rite" that is often hardly recognizable.

[45] Turner, "Ritual", 525. A similar analysis is presented by Hitchcock, *Recovery of the Sacred*, in the chapter entitled "The Death of Community", 74–96. See also the trenchant sociological critique of A. Archer, *The Two Catholic Churches: A Study in Oppression* (London: SCM Press, 1986).

[46] Although a mentality of liturgical "lawlessness" has contributed to the present predicament. This problem is addressed by the Congregation for Divine Worship and the Discipline of the Sacraments in the Instruction *Redemptionis Sacramentum* on Certain Matters to Be Observed or to Be Avoided regarding the Most Holy Eucharist (March 25, 2004).

Liminality and Communitas

Turner extols the traditional Roman Rite for allowing its participants to enter the state of "liminality", literally "being-on-a-threshold", where "they cease to be bounded by the secular structures of their own age and confront eternity which is equidistant from all ages".[47] What makes his analysis so interesting for this study is the fact that he arrives at a description of the "sacred" that goes beyond the simple antithesis between sacred and profane of Durkheim, Otto, or Eliade. As has already been seen, he is emphatic that ritual and its symbolism are not simply the expression, reflection, or projection of social structure, as some social anthropologists have postulated. Rather, he sees the function of ritual "partly to protect and partly to express truths which make men free from the exigencies of their status incumbencies, free to contemplate and pray as well as to speculate and invent".[48] Essential for understanding his theory are the two key concepts of the liminal or liminality, that is, the passage between social experiences, a state "betwixt and between", and *communitas* (Turner uses the Latin term), which is a description of society or community as a reality that is not restricted to socio-economic structures. The ritual forms of *communitas* are essentially egalitarian and subvert, or at least suspend, secular distinctions of status and role. In certain ritual situations, Turner observes, even persons who are profoundly separated from one another in the ordinary world, "cooperate closely to ensure what is believed to be the maintenance of a cosmic order which transcends the contradictions and conflicts inherent in the mundane social

[47] Turner, "Ritual", 524.

[48] Turner, "Passages, Margins, and Poverty", 391.

system".[49] This is not to say that there is no structure in *communitas*; but this is not a social structure that is recognized and operative in a society. Rather, it is "a structure of symbols and ideas", or, as Turner adds, an "instructional" structure. In terms of the French anthropologist Claude Lévi-Strauss, it is

> a way of inscribing in the mentalities of neophytes generative rules, codes, and media whereby they can manipulate the symbols of speech and culture to confer some degree of intelligibility on an "experience" that "perpetually outstrips the possibilities of linguistic (and other cultural) expression".[50]

It is instructive to compare Turner's theory with the claim of the volume *Ritual and Its Consequences: An Essay on the Limits of Sincerity*, jointly written by a group of scholars in religion, anthropology, and psychoanalysis, that ritual creates a subjunctive universe, a shared "as if" or "could be", which creates a temporal order within the ambiguities of social relationships. The authors propose a wide conception of ritual that is not limited to religious or even secular ritual. The examples of saying "please" and "thank you" or of asking "How are you?" (a question to which no sincere answer is expected) illustrate how everyday ritual constructs equality between people, which may not represent actual socioeconomic structures but establishes an order of civility and

[49] Ibid., 398. Cf. Turner's seminal work, *The Ritual Process: Structure and Anti-Structure*, with a foreword by R. D. Abrahams (Piscataway, N.J.: Aldine Transaction, 1969; second printing, 2008).

[50] Turner, "Passages, Margins, and Poverty", 400. The single quotes are given in the article without footnote. The quote may be taken from the earlier referenced C. Lévi-Strauss, *Structural Anthropology*, trans. C. Jacobson and B. Grundfest Schoepf (New York: Basic Books 1963).

politeness.[51] The working of ritual is thus conceived in a way that is not unlike Turner's description of liminality as being "similar to the subjunctive mood in verbs";[52] the crucial difference, however, is the authors' apparent rejection, if not denunciation, of any realist position. The "as if" of ritual is an illusion that helps us to negotiate our boundaries and get on with one another in a broken and ambiguous world; hence it is necessary work, to be repeated over and over, but how can it achieve this if it is completely detached from reality "as it is" (or "as it should be")? By contrast, for Turner, religious ritual is representative of a cosmic order and allows its participants to integrate their experience of the human condition into this order.

In his studies on liminality and *communitas*, Turner has arrived at a complex description of the sacred that moves beyond the simple contrast with the profane and accounts for the important role of ritual. Persons who are involved in the socio-economic structure of their society are constrained by its rules, conditioned by its values, and pressured by its conflicts. This is the sphere of the ordinary or quotidian, which, especially in its contemporary secularist form, leaves little space for the contemplation of the transcendent. In ritual liminality, however, the same persons

> are placed, so to speak, outside the total system and its conflicts; transiently, they become men apart—and it is

[51] A. B. Seligman, R. P. Weller, M. J. Puett, and B. Simon, *Ritual and Its Consequences: An Essay on the Limits of Sincerity* (New York: Oxford University Press, 2008), 7–8.

[52] V. Turner, "Frame, Flow and Reflection: Ritual and Drama as Public Liminality", *Japanese Journal of Religious Studies* 6 (1979): 465–99, at 465. The main themes of *Ritual and Its Consequences* are already presented by Turner in this study, including the importance of "framing" for the process of ritualization.

surprising how often the term "sacred" may be translated as "set apart" or "on one side" in various societies.[53]

In some respects, the difference between Durkheim (and his followers) and Turner is like the difference between the understanding of the sacred prevalent in classical antiquity, reclaimed in modernity, and that of Christianity. What was truly sacred for Greco-Roman civilization (with the notable exception of the philosophers) was the city, not the temple; religious ritual was an extension of the city and its power and could be conceived as no more than a civic instrument. The transpolitical religion of Christianity changes this, which is why its rituals provide a transcendence from social structures rather than a reinforcement of them.[54]

Liminality has its own time and space, which are framed in such a way that they are set off from the routine world. Ritual so conceived requires forms of expression that are different from those of the social structures. Hence they can never be entirely "contemporary". Some of these forms will be inherited and archaic, but they will be "alive" inasmuch as they are, in Turner's words, "the product . . . of liminality and communitas (between man and God as well as between man and man)". This is one of the essential characteristics of what we mean by rite in a Catholic theological perspective. And Turner adds: "Archaic patterns of actions and objects which arose in the past from the free space within liminality can become protective of future free spaces. The archaic is not the obsolete."[55] This needs to be remembered in the

[53] Turner, "Passages, Margins, and Poverty", 401.

[54] I gratefully owe this observation to Michael P. Foley.

[55] Turner, "Passages, Margins, and Poverty", 391.

chapters that will be dedicated to the question of which architectural, artistic, and musical forms are adequate for the sacred liturgy.

II

The Sacred in Contemporary Catholic Theology

The previous chapter has shown the sacred as a well-established category in social anthropology and ritual studies. Moving beyond a simple antithesis between sacred and profane, Victor Turner has presented the sacred as a suspension or even subversion of the ordinary or quotidian world of socio-economic structures by setting persons apart and placing them in the realm of ritual liminality and *communitas*. This shared ritual experience enables them to integrate their experience of the human condition in all its fragility and ambiguity into a cosmic order and so make sense of it. It may therefore come as a surprise that a major strand in twentieth-century Catholic theology has contested the validity of the concept of the sacred in Christianity. It will be necessary to understand the arguments presented in favor of this position and to explore ways of responding to it cogently.

Calling the Sacred into Question: Edward Schillebeeckx and Karl Rahner

The sacred in Christianity has been called into question by a liturgical and sacramental theology grounded in the writings of the Belgian Dominican Edward Schillebeeckx and the German Jesuit Karl Rahner.[1] To put it succinctly, even at the risk of unduly simplifying matters, it can be said that in this vision the whole created world is regarded as already endowed with or permeated by divine grace. As Schillebeeckx writes in his widely received book *Christ the Sacrament of the Encounter with God*, "the whole created world becomes, through Christ's incarnation and the God-man relationship which is consequent upon it, an outward grace, an offer of grace in sacramental form".[2] Such a reading of the Incarnation raises the question of the distinctiveness of the Church's sacraments in the communication of divine grace. While the early Schillebeeckx's sacramental theology is still indebted to a Thomistic Christology and ecclesiology, in his later writings the sacraments appear to be subsumed into the general category of rituals that lead to an existential encounter with God.[3]

Schillebeeckx had a notable influence on the development of Rahner's theology. According to Patrick Burke, Rahner, from the early 1960s, "although never actually denying the grace-nature distinction, stresses ever more their existential unity and (. . .) begins to see categorical revelation as only the posterior explicitization of what man always and originally is".[4] This idea of transcendental revelation provides

[1] Cf. D. A. Stosur, *The Theology of Liturgical Blessing in the Book of Blessings: A Phenomenologico-Theological Investigation of a Liturgical Book* (Ph.D. dissertation, University of Notre Dame, 1994), who, unlike the present writer, is wholly positive in his evaluation of this school of thought.

[2] E. Schillebeeckx, *Christ, the Sacrament of the Encounter with God* (New York: Sheed and Ward, 1963), 216. This was published originally as *Christus, Sacrament van de Godsontmoeting* (Bilthoven: H. Nelissen, 1960), which is a shorter version of *De sacramentele Heilseconomie*, published in 1952.

[3] See J. Geldhof, "The Early and Late Schillebeeckx OP on Rituals, Liturgies, and Sacraments", *Usus Antiquior* 1 (2010): 132–50, at 140.

[4] P. Burke, *Reinterpreting Rahner: A Critical Study of His Major Themes* (New York: Fordham University Press, 2002), 47–48. For recent critical reflections

the foundation for the later theory of the anonymous Christian; the consequence Rahner draws for his understanding of grace is that he "sees it coming to categorical expression in any categorical experience, even if not specifically Christian or even religious".[5]

Consequently, the notion of "sacramentality" is extended to such a degree that the Church's sacraments are considered nothing more than manifestations, albeit significant ones, that make explicit what already takes place in the world. In 1970, Rahner writes that

> the sacraments constitute the manifestation of the holiness and the redeemed state of the secular dimension of human life and of the world. Man does not enter a temple, a fane which encloses the holy and cuts it off from a godless and secular world which remains outside. Rather in the free breadth of a divine world he erects a landmark, a sign of the fact that this entire world belongs to God, a sign precisely of the fact that God is adored, experienced and accepted everywhere as he who, through his "grace", has himself set all things free to attain to himself, and a sign that this adoration of him takes place not in Jerusalem alone but everywhere in spirit and in truth.[6]

---

on Rahner's theology, see also M. Hauke, "Karl Rahner nella critica di Leo Scheffczyk", in *Karl Rahner: Un'analisi critica: La figura, l'opera e la recezione teologica di Karl Rahner (1904–1984)*, ed. S. M. Lanzetta (Siena: Cantagalli, 2009), 267–87. M. Gagliardi, *Liturgia fonte di vita* (Verona: Fede & Cultura, 2009), 58–73.

[5] Burke, *Reinterpreting Rahner*, 246.

[6] K. Rahner, "Considerations on the Active Role of the Person in the Sacramental Event", in Rahner, *Theological Investigations*, vol. 14: *Ecclesiology, Questions in the Church, the Church in the World*, trans. D. Bourke (New York: Seabury Press, 1976), 161–84 ("Überlegungen zum personalen Vollzug des sakramentalen Geschehens", in *Schriften zur Theologie*, vol. 10 [Einsiedeln: Benziger, 1972], 405–29, originally published in 1970), at 169.

In this reading, worship "in spirit and truth", announced by Christ in his encounter with the Samaritan woman at the well of Jacob (Jn 4:23–24), overcomes any separation between the sacred and the secular or profane. As a consequence, the experience and acceptance of God's redemption cannot be limited to specific ritual expressions. Unlike classical theology, then, the sacraments are not taken as sacred signs that confer the grace they signify or instrumental causes of grace *extra nos* but, rather, as visible manifestations of the inner event of grace that is already taking place in man and in the world and is not necessarily linked with Christian revelation. Rahner himself speaks of a "Copernican turn" in sacramental theology.[7] The sacrament, as conventionally understood, is "a small sign" that reminds us of the infinite presence of God's grace in the world and, by means of this memorial (*anamnesis*), becomes an event of the same grace. Although Rahner adds that this sign is "necessary, reasonable and indispensable", it is not intelligible why this should be so.[8] At this point Teilhard de Chardin's idea of the "liturgy of the world" is introduced:

> The world and its history are the sublime liturgy, breathing of death and sacrifice, which God celebrates and causes to be celebrated in and through human history in its freedom, this being something which he in turn sustains in grace by his sovereign disposition.[9]

[7] This idea is already contained in Rahner's article "Sakrament: V. Systematik", in *Lexikon für Theologie und Kirche* (2nd ed.), vol. 9 (1964), 227–30, at 228, and more clearly articulated in his "Kleine Vorüberlegung über die Sakramente im allgemeinen", in Rahner, *Über die Sakramente der Kirche: Meditationen* (Freiburg: Herder, 1985), 11–21 (originally published in 1974).

[8] Rahner, "Considerations on the Active Role", 169.

[9] Ibid., 170.

What is described here is a kind of primordial (Eucharistic) liturgy, which is reflected in "that which we are accustomed to call liturgy in the more usual sense".[10] In other words, sacramental celebrations symbolize the "liturgy of the world" that is already taking place. On a rather apologetic note, Rahner adds that this conception does not lessen the importance of liturgy in its traditional sense.[11]

From a Rahnerian perspective, then, a distinction between the sacred and the non-sacred (however the categories may actually be defined) hardly makes sense. Rather, I would argue, the sacred merges into the infinite horizon of God's grace already present in the world. A theological response to Rahner needs first of all to acknowledge the legitimacy in rejecting a radical separation between the sacred and the profane as postulated by sociologists such as Durkheim and religious phenomenologists such as Otto and Eliade. Josef Pieper rightly observes that the contrast or distinction between the sacred and the ordinary or quotidian is valid "*within* one common and comprehensive reality". To illustrate his argument, Pieper adduces two analogies: "Poetry and prose are but two different modes of speaking about what is real . . . and philosophy no less than science attempts to know and understand the vast subject matter called 'reality.'"[12]

[10] Ibid. Cf. the well-researched if rather uncritical study of M. Skelley, *The Liturgy of the World: Karl Rahner's Theology of Worship*, foreword by R. G. Weakland (Collegeville, Minn.: Liturgical Press, 1991).

[11] K. Rahner, "On the Theology of Worship", in Rahner, *Theological Investigations*, vol. 19: *Faith and Ministry*, trans. E. Quinn (New York: Crossroad, 1983), 141–49 ("Zur Theologie des Gottesdienstes", in *Schriften zur Theologie*, vol. 14 [Einsiedeln: Benziger, 1980], 227–37, originally published in 1979), at 142–43.

[12] J. Pieper, *In Search of the Sacred*, trans. L. Krauth (San Francisco: Ignatius Press, 1991), 20.

Secondly, it needs to be recognized that experience of the sacred is always *mediated* in some form. Direct access to the divine, as in mystical phenomena, is extremely rare. Thus Jean-Paul Audet, speaking of "solidarity between the sacred and the profane (*solidarité du sacré et du profane*)", argues that the ways and means of this mediation partake in the divine reality and are made sacred because of this participation.[13] Such attention to the mediation of the sacred is obviously pertinent when we consider the liturgy and its forms of expression. To a certain extent, then, Rahner's critique is to the point and needs to be heeded, but at the same time there are fundamental flaws in this approach that were identified at an early stage of the debate by Louis Bouyer.[14] Bouyer identifies two contrary tendencies in the liturgical theology of his time and sees them connected with erroneous understandings of the Incarnation that fueled the christological controversies in the fourth and fifth century. On the one hand, there is a school of thought that considers the liturgy in all its forms and expressions as equally sacred and therefore immutable. Bouyer compares this position to Monophysitism, the theological position that tends to absorb Christ's humanity into his divinity. The human aspect of the liturgy is ignored or even denied, and so is its historical growth and development, with the possibility of ongoing renewal.

On the other hand, there is an overemphasis on the human aspects of the liturgy, which Bouyer compares to a Nestorian

[13] J.-P. Audet, "Le sacré e le profane: leur situation en christianisme", *Nouvelle Revue théologique* 79 (1957): 33–61.

[14] See L. Bouyer, *Rite and Man: The Sense of the Sacral and Christian Liturgy*, trans. M.J. Costelloe (London: Burns & Oates, 1963), 8–10. The original French edition was published in 1962. The introduction, in which these observations are found, was published separately as "Two Temptations", *Worship* 37 (1962): 11–21.

separation of Christ's humanity from his divine person. This idea is first detected in the assimilation of Christian rites to the patterns of pagan "mystery religions". With the stress on the common experiences of the sacred in humanity, the specific character of Christian revelation and its newness are not sufficiently recognized. This critique is specifically aimed at the mystery theology of Odo Casel.[15]

Bouyer also identifies a second strand of liturgical "Nestorianism"; although he does not give names, his account corresponds to the theological conception of the sacred developed by Schillebeeckx and Rahner, which I have just analyzed. There is some merit in this conception, insofar as it would seem to respond to a theory, such as Casel's, that tends to merge or even confuse the sacred in Christianity with pre-Christian ideas of the sacred. The strength of this response lies thus in its grasp of the Gospel's originality and in its conviction that, precisely because of this originality, the Christian faith can speak to the contemporary, secular world. However, this approach goes too far in rejecting all sacrality in the ordinary sense of the word and in maintaining that Christianity has nothing in common with it. According to this interpretation, the separation of the sacred and profane is overcome by the Incarnation of the Word, which consecrated humanity—and the world—in its "profaneness". From there often follows a denunciation of the development of ritual that began already in early Christianity.

While it is true that the totality of human life is to be permeated by the presence of Christ, it would be mistaken to believe "that a salvation of humanity means to leave it as it is, and even to wipe out all distinctions between the sacred

[15] As Bouyer makes clear later in *Rite and Man*, 34–37.

and the profane in order to allow it to be simply itself while belonging wholly to God in Christ".[16] Bouyer continues:

> The "Law of the Incarnation" which they advance is not actually what they believe it to be, that is, the assumption of profane humanity *en bloc* so as to consecrate it with no other change than an illumination of its profound nature through grace. Quite the contrary, the "Law of the Incarnation" consists in producing a new sacrality, a renewed consecration, by the setting aside of a humanity which, in order to belong wholly to God, does not at all belong to itself. Such is in fact the humanity of the God made man, and it is because of this that it can save us. In this way, and only in this way, as St. Paul declares, is there prepared a final consecration of the whole of humanity in the body of Christ.[17]

No reference is given to the Pauline passages Bouyer has in mind here, but one could think of Romans 15:16, where the apostle declares "to be a minister of Christ Jesus to the Gentiles in the priestly service of the gospel of God, so that the offering of the Gentiles may be acceptable, sanctified by the Holy Spirit".

Bouyer was inclined to express his positions sharply, and his taste for polemics made him at times overstate the good case he had. However, he clearly identifies the problems with contemporary theological approaches to the sacred and so clears the ground for its reappraisal.

Recovering the Sacred: Julien Ries and Joseph Ratzinger

An important contribution toward such a reappraisal has been made by the Belgian religious historian and anthropo-

[16] Ibid., 9–10.
[17] Ibid, 10.

logist Julien Ries (created a cardinal by Pope Benedict XVI on February 18, 2012). With reference to the exegetical work of Pierre Grelot, Ries notes the originality of the Christian conception of the sacred, which can be understood only in relation to the person of Jesus Christ.[18]

A frequent theme in the Old Testament is God's holiness, for instance, in the *Trisagion* of Isaiah 6:3, "Holy, holy, holy is the LORD of hosts" (taken up in Rev 4:8). In fact, God alone is called the "Holy One" (*qadoš*) in the full sense of the word. "Holiness" is a quality that belongs above all to God and describes his being divine; in its mature form, it expresses God's otherness or transcendence. In the long discourse that is contained in chapter 17 of Saint John's Gospel and known as his high-priestly prayer, Jesus invokes his "holy Father" (Jn 17:11) in line with the conception of the Hebrew Scriptures. There is, however, an important difference here, in that the enormous distance between God and man, which is implied in Isaiah's proclamation of God's all-surpassing holiness, is *mediated* by sending his Son into the world. Thus God comes close to his people and calls them to communion with himself. God's holiness is not simply made manifest in Christ but also communicated to the world in him.

At a significant moment in the high-priestly prayer, Jesus asks his heavenly Father with regard to his disciples: "Sanctify them in the truth; your word is truth . . . For their sake I consecrate myself, that they also may be consecrated in truth" (Jn 17:17, 19). Earlier in the same Gospel, Jesus speaks of himself as the one "whom the Father consecrated and sent into the world" (Jn 10:36). In the second volume

[18] J. Ries, "*Homo religiosus*, sacré, sainteté", in *L'expression du sacré dans les grandes religions. III: Mazdéisme, cultes isiaques, religion grecque, Manichéisme, Nouveau Testament, vie de l'Homo religiosus*, ed. J. Ries, Homo religiosus 3 (Louvain-la-Neuve: Centre d'Histoire des Religions, 1986), 331–84, esp. 373–81.

of his book *Jesus of Nazareth*, Benedict XVI comments on the meaning of "consecrate" or "sanctify" (both words translate the same Greek verb *hagiázein*), which he reads in "connection with the event of atonement and with the high priesthood".[19]

The meaning of "sanctify" here is rooted in the Hebrew conception of God as the "Holy One" and, hence, means "handing over a reality—a person or even a thing—to God, especially through appropriation for worship".[20] This can happen in preparing and offering sacrifice to God (cf. Ex 12:3; Deut 15:19) or in consecration for priesthood (cf. Ex 28:41). According to Benedict XVI, the process of "sanctification" or "consecration" of which Jesus speaks in the high-priestly prayer comprises two aspects that only appear to be opposed but are in fact two aspects of the same complex reality. On the one hand, consecration means "setting apart from the rest of reality that pertains to man's ordinary everyday life". The person or object that is consecrated is handed over entirely to God and hence is no longer under human control. On the other hand, such consecration al-

[19] J. Ratzinger (Benedict XVI), *Jesus of Nazareth. Part Two: Holy Week: From the Entrance into Jerusalem to the Resurrection*, trans. P. J. Whitmore (San Francisco: Ignatius Press, 2011), 85; see also the pope's *Homily for the Chrism Mass* (April 9, 2009). Benedict XVI relies on A. Feuillet, *Le sacerdoce du Christ et de ses ministres d'après la prière sacerdotale du quatrième Évangile et plusieurs données parallèles du Nouveau Testament* (1972; Paris: Téqui, 1997). Feuillet's reading, while not being generally accepted by biblical scholars today, is already attested in some early Church Fathers; cf. the brief discussion by J. Zumstein, *L'Évangile selon saint Jean (13–21)*, Commentaire du Nouveau Testament, 2nd series, IVb (Geneva: Labor et Fides, 2007), 180.

[20] Ratzinger, *Jesus of Nazareth*, 86. In the German original, the word *heiligen* is used for *hagiázein* and is then explained in its twofold meaning as *heiligen* and *weihen*: *Jesus von Nazareth. Zweiter Teil: Vom Einzug in Jerusalem bis zur Auferstehung* (Freiburg: Herder, 2011), 104. The fact that the same Greek verb is translated differently is significant: the sense of *hagiázein* in John 17 is not restricted to moral holiness or to a dedication to a particular mission but indicates, rather, a more profound dimension of consecration.

ways includes "the essential dynamic of 'existing for'": precisely because it is handed over into the sphere of God, the consecrated reality exists now for the world and for its salvation.[21] These two aspects of consecration are only seemingly contrary to each other, as is shown by the three moments of consecration of which Jesus speaks in John's Gospel.

The first consecration, that of the Son by the Father, is identified with the Incarnation. Peter confesses Jesus as "the Holy One of God" in the synagogue of Capernaum (Jn 6:69), and by applying this title, which the Old Testament reserves to God alone, to Jesus, as is done in other New Testament passages as well,[22] Peter professes his divinity. As the Holy One of God, Jesus belongs totally to God, and at the same time, in his Incarnation, he is sent into the world and exists for it. His "holiness" is at the heart of his messianic mission.

The second consecration is indicated when Christ speaks of consecrating himself. In his exegesis of this passage, the biblical scholar Rudolf Bultmann noted the temporal vicinity of this so-called farewell discourse with the beginning of Christ's Passion. Moreover, this act of consecration or sanctification (the Greek *hagiázein*) is made "for their sake" (*hypèr autōn*), thus giving it a sacrificial dimension. This second consecration anticipates the Christ's offering of himself on the Cross. Bultmann also sees in this an allusion to the words of the Last Supper.[23]

[21] Ratzinger, *Jesus of Nazareth*, 86. This connection is seen in "the special vocation of Israel: on the one hand, it is set apart from all other peoples, but for a particular reason—in order to carry out a commission for all people, for the whole world. That is what is meant when Israel is designated a 'holy people'": ibid.

[22] Mk 1:24, Lk 1:35, Acts 4:27 and 30.

[23] R. Bultmann, *Das Evangelium des Johannes*, Meyers kritisch-exegetischer Kommentar über das Neue Testament, 2, 21st ed. (Göttingen: Vandenhoeck & Ruprecht, 1986), 391n3; cf. Feuillet, *Sacerdoce du Christ*, 31 and 38; Ratzinger, *Jesus of Nazareth*, 87–88.

In the reading of Benedict XVI, the ritual background of the high-priestly prayer of Jesus is a hermeneutical key. The setting in which this important Gospel text is presented is the great Day of Atonement, which is renewed in the new liturgy of atonement, of which Jesus himself is the high priest, "sent into the world by the Father"; at the same time he is the victim, "made present in the Eucharist of all times".[24] The inner meaning of the Day of Atonement is thus fulfilled in the Incarnation of the Eternal Word "for the life of the world" (Jn 6:51). From the moment that Jesus comes into this world in human flesh, he is consecrated priest to offer sacrifice and to intercede for his people, and this consecration is perfected in his Passion and Cross. The messianic mission of Christ thus also has a ritual dimension, and its focal point is the priesthood of Christ, the mediator between God and man.

The third consecration consists in the disciples' participation in the consecration of Christ according to the two aspects already mentioned. The disciples are appropriated into God's sphere, and, at the same time, they are sent into the world to fulfill a priestly mission. This third consecration of John 17 is important because it not only presents the consecration of Jesus Christ as priest, as does the Letter to the Hebrews in language that draws on Temple worship,[25] but also includes the participation of the apostles in this consecration. For this reason Benedict XVI recognizes in this Gospel passage the priesthood of the New Testament, which is nothing else but a participation in the

[24] Ratzinger, *Jesus of Nazareth*, 88.

[25] Christ is "high priest of the good things that have come" (Heb 9:11) and "the mediator of a new covenant" (Heb 9:15), established in his blood, which purifies our "conscience from dead works" (Heb 9:14).

priesthood of Jesus Christ, the one high priest of the New Covenant.[26]

The Sacredness of the Liturgy

These biblical reflections on the meaning of "consecration" or "sanctification" in Saint John's Gospel enable us to take a fresh look at the theme of the "sacredness" of the liturgy. The hermeneutical key for this enquiry will be *Sacrosanctum Concilium*'s definition of the liturgy as "an exercise of the priestly office [*munus*] of Jesus Christ". The conciliar Constitution on the Sacred Liturgy goes on to say:

> In the liturgy the sanctification of man is signified by signs perceptible to the senses, and is effected in a way which corresponds with each of these signs; in the liturgy the whole public worship is performed by the Mystical Body of Jesus Christ, that is, by the Head and His members.[27]

This passage restates a key principle of Catholic worship, formulated by Saint Thomas Aquinas,[28] proclaimed in a very similar way by Pope Pius XII in his encyclical *Mediator Dei*,[29] and resumed in the *Catechism of the Catholic*

[26] Cf. Ratzinger, *Jesus of Nazareth*, 90; *Homily for the Chrism Mass* (April 9, 2009).

[27] Second Vatican Council, Constitution on the Sacred Liturgy *Sacrosanctum Concilium* (December 4, 1963), no. 7.

[28] Thomas Aquinas, *Summa Theologiae* III, q. 63, a. 3: "Now the whole rite of the Christian religion is derived from Christ's priesthood (*Totus autem ritus christianae religionis derivatur a sacerdotio Christi*)". English translation of *Summa* here and in the following by the Fathers of the English Dominican Province, online edition (www.newadvent.org/summa/).

[29] Pius XII, Encyclical Letter on the Sacred Liturgy *Mediator Dei* (November 20, 1947), no. 20: "The sacred liturgy is, consequently, the public worship which our Redeemer as Head of the Church renders to the Father, as well

Church.[30] In these magisterial documents, the liturgy is seen as the exercise of the priesthood of Christ; to be more precise, of *Christus totus* (following the principle that guided Saint Augustine's exegesis, especially of the Psalms): the whole Christ, the Head and the members of his Mystical Body, which is the Church. Those who participate in this exercise of Christ's priesthood are the ordained priest, who acts in the person of Christ the Head (*in persona Christi capitis*) by virtue of his priestly ordination, and the baptized faithful as members of the Mystical Body. Note that at *this* point, *Sacrosanctum Concilium* introduces the notion of the sacredness of the liturgy, when it explains:

> From this it follows that every liturgical celebration, because it is an action of Christ the priest and of His Body which is the Church, is a sacred action surpassing all others; no other action of the Church can equal its efficacy by the same title and to the same degree.[31]

In other words, *Sacrosanctum Concilium* considers "sacredness" always derived from the liturgy, which is the presence and action of Christ in his Mystical Body. This follows the principle formulated by Saint Thomas Aquinas that we call a thing sacred (*sacrum*) because of its relation to divine wor-

---

as the worship which the community of the faithful renders to its Founder, and through Him to the heavenly Father. It is, in short, the worship rendered by the Mystical Body of Christ in the entirety of its Head and members." Ibid., no. 22: "Thenceforth the priesthood of Jesus Christ is a living and continuous reality through all the ages to the end of time, since the liturgy is nothing more nor less than the exercise of this priestly function."

[30] Cf. *Catechism of the Catholic Church*, 2nd ed. (Washington, D.C.: United States Catholic Conference, 2000), nos. 1066–70, and, in a condensed way, *Compendium: Catechism of the Catholic Church* (Washington, D.C.: United States Conference of Catholic Bishops, 2006), no. 218.

[31] *Sacrosanctum Concilium*, no. 7.

ship (*ad cultum divinum*).[32] This would confirm the insight gained in the previous chapter that ritual has an active role in framing the sacred and setting it apart from the quotidian. Josef Pieper, who wrote on the subject at a time when it was fiercely contested, argues that this concept of the sacred is widely confirmed by ethnology and philosophy of religion, "and no less by the theological interpretation of the Old and New Testaments".[33] He also records a use of language that points to an essential characteristic of the liturgy: it is never simply "done", but is "celebrated". Both in classical and Christian liturgical sources, the verb *celebrare* means "carrying out an action in a nonordinary manner, on the part of the community".[34] Moreover, unlike personal and interior prayer, the liturgy is an external action, which has its concrete and material forms of expressions, in which the human senses are always involved. Public worship thus is in need of its proper place, its proper time, and its proper objects that are specifically dedicated so that it can be celebrated as a sacred action. It is in relation to this sacred action that we also speak of sacred space, sacred time, or sacred objects.

Regarding sacred objects, William P. Mahrt perceptively notes "two complementary aspects: an intrinsic suitability or aptness to the sacred purpose, and a process of being

[32] Thomas Aquinas, *Summa Theologiae* II-II, q. 99, a. 1, co.; cf. II-II, q. 81, a. 8, co.: "Not only men, but also the temple, vessels and such like things are said to be sanctified through being applied to the worship of God." See also I-II, q. 101, a. 4, on the "sacred things" of the ceremonial precepts under the Old Law.

[33] Pieper, *In Search of the Sacred*, 25; see also "Sakralität und 'Entsakralisierung' (1969)", in Pieper, *Werke*, vol. 7: *Religionsphilosophische Schriften*, ed. B. Wald (Hamburg: Felix Meiner, 2000), 394–419, at 403–4.

[34] Pieper, *In Search of the Sacred*, 26, with reference to B. Droste, "Celebrare" in der römischen Liturgiesprache (Munich: Hueber, 1963), 196.

received as sacred".[35] The process of reception can take the form of gradual acceptance or of immemorial convention. An example of gradual acceptance is the chasuble as a liturgical vestment: this was originally the common outer garment worn by well-to-do Roman citizens in late antiquity (*paenula*). Initially, its liturgical use was distinguished by the material quality of a specific vestment and by its being set aside for worship. However, the chasuble proved to be intrinsically suitable for sacred use because it covers the bishop or priest completely and so draws attention to his acting *in persona Christi* rather than to his individuality. An example of immemorial convention would be the use of incense; its rare origin, sweet-smelling perfume, and high-ascending smoke easily make it particularly appropriate for liturgical worship. Although it was rejected in earliest Christianity because of its pagan connotations, it was eventually adopted as a symbol of the prayers of the faithful rising to God.[36]

There is another fundamental argument to consider here: from the Christian perspective, the sacredness of the liturgy is based on its sacramental character. When *Sacrosanctum Concilium* affirms that in the liturgy, which is the exercise of the priesthood of Christ, the sanctification of man is signified and at the same time effected by signs perceptible to the senses,[37] it obviously refers to the sacraments. Now, the essential rites of the sacraments—form and matter in Scholastic terminology—are distinguished by a stupendous

[35] W. P. Mahrt, "Music and the Sacrality of the Two Forms", in *Benedict XVI and the Roman Missal: Proceedings of the Fourth Fota International Liturgical Conference*, 2011, ed. J. E. Rutherford and J. O'Brien, Fota Liturgy Series (Dublin and New York: Four Courts Press and Scepter Publishers, 2013), 192–207, at 194.

[36] See ibid., 194–95.

[37] *Sacrosanctum Concilium*, no. 7.

humility and simplicity. The liturgy, as sacred action, surrounds these essential rites with other rites and ceremonies that illustrate them and help the faithful to a better understanding of the great mystery that is made present.[38] The reality of the sacraments, which is veiled and hidden to the senses, is translated into signs that are perceptible and hence more easily accessible to our understanding. The purpose of this is that the Christian community, "instructed by the sacred actions (*sacris actionibus erudita*)", as an ancient prayer in the *Gregorian Sacramentary* says, be properly disposed to receive God's grace and blessing.[39] The sacred character of the liturgy can thus be seen as part of a divine pedagogy.

For Thomas Aquinas, the elements of human institution

[38] See Council of Trent, session 22 (1562), *Doctrine on the Sacrifice of the Mass*, chap. 5: "On the Solemn Ceremonies of the Sacrifice of the Mass", H. Denzinger, *Enchiridion Symbolorum: Compendium of Creeds, Definitions, and Declarations of the Catholic Church*, ed. P. Hünermann, H. Hoping, R. Fastiggi, and A. Englund Nash, 43rd ed. (San Francisco: Ignatius Press, 2012), no. 1746: "And as human nature is such that it cannot easily raise itself up to the meditation of divine realities without external aids, Holy Mother Church has for that reason duly established certain rites . . . and . . . has provided ceremonial . . . such as mystical blessings, lights, incense, vestments, and many other rituals of that kind from apostolic order and tradition, by which the majesty of this great sacrifice is enhanced and the minds of the faithful are aroused by those visible signs of religious devotion to contemplation of the high mysteries hidden in this sacrifice."

[39] *Sacramentarium Gregorianum* (Hadrianum), nos. 308, 895: ed. J. Deshusses, *Le sacramentaire grégorien: Ses principales formes d'après les plus anciens manuscrits*, vol. 1, Spicilegium Friburgense 16, 3rd ed. (Fribourg: Éditions Universitaires, 1992). In *Missale Romanum ex decreto SS. Concilii Tridentini restitutum Summorum Pontificum cura recognitum*, editio typica (Vatican City: Typis Polyglottis Vaticanis, 1962), the prayer is used as the Collect for the Saturday after Passion Sunday: "Proficiat, quaesumus, Domine, plebs tibi dicata piae devotionis affectu: ut, sacris actionibus erudita, quanto maiestati tuae fit gratior, tanto donis potioribus augeatur (May the people dedicated to you, Lord, we pray, advance in piety and devotion, so that, instructed by the sacred actions, they may abound in ever greater gifts, as they become more pleasing to your majesty)."

in the sacraments, while not being essential to them, belong to the "solemnity" (*solemnitas*) that serves to awaken devotion and reverence in those who receive it, especially in the Most Holy Eucharist.[40] Pieper proposes a broad definition of "sacred language", which includes signs and gestures as well as the words used in public worship. In a similar way, the English Dominican Aidan Nichols speaks of "the idiom of worship"; both concepts are by no means restricted to the linguistic aspects of the liturgy and cover more or less the same ground as Aquinas' idea of *solemnitas*.[41] I would therefore propose to see in the sacrality of the liturgy the expression of its sacramentality. Consequently, the question needs to be asked whether Catholic theologians who have endorsed the movements toward a "desacralization" have a strong enough sense of the sacramental principle. It has been Pieper's argument that such theologies "are ultimately rooted" in a "denial of any sacramental reality".[42]

In his book on *The Spirit of the Liturgy*, Joseph Ratzinger offers another perspective on the meaning of the sacred in Christianity when he responds to theological critics of the

[40] Thomas Aquinas, *Summa Theologiae* III, q. 64, a. 2 ad 1: "Human institutions observed in the sacraments are not essential to the sacrament; but belong to the solemnity which is added to the sacraments in order to arouse devotion and reverence in the recipients." See also III, q. 83, a. 4, co.: "Since the whole mystery of our salvation is comprised in this sacrament, therefore is it performed with greater solemnity than the other sacraments", and III, q. 66, a. 10, co., on the ceremonies of the rite of baptism. Cf. T. A. Becker, "The Role of *Solemnitas* in the Liturgy according to Saint Thomas Aquinas", in *Rediscovering Aquinas and the Sacraments: Studies in Sacramental Theology*, ed. M. Levering and M. Dauphinais (Chicago: Hillenbrand, 2009), 114–35.

[41] See Pieper, "Sakralität und 'Entsakralisierung' (1969)" and *In Search of the Sacred, passim*; A. Nichols, *Looking at the Liturgy: A Critical View of Its Contemporary Form* (San Francisco: Ignatius Press, 1996), 87–114.

[42] Pieper, *In Search of the Sacred*, 29; cf. "Sakralität und Entsakralisierung", 406.

idea that there should be any such thing as "sacred time" and "sacred space" for Christians. Their critique takes as a scriptural basis Christ's announcement in Saint John's Gospel of a worship "in spirit and truth" (Jn 4:23–24), a passage also invoked by Rahner in the text quoted above. This is correctly taken to mean "the transition from Temple sacrifice to universal worship"; it would be erroneous, however, to draw the consequence that such universal worship is no longer bound by the frames and boundaries of the sacred. The cardinal recalls that we live in the time of "not yet", that is, we have not yet passed over to the New Jerusalem, where God himself and the Lamb are its Temple (Rev 21:22–23). Certainly, with the revelation of the Son of God, this new reality has entered our world, but only in an inchoative way, like at "the time of dawn, when darkness and light are intermingled", as Joseph Ratzinger explains with reference to the commentary of Saint Gregory the Great on the apostle Paul's word, "The night is far gone, the day is at hand" (Rom 13:12). This is the time of the Church, which is an intermediate state between "already" and "not yet". In this state, the "empirical conditions of life in this world are still in force", and for this reason the distinction between the sacred and the quotidian still hold, even if this distinction is not conceived of as an absolute separation. With the Church Fathers, this time can be described as "image between shadow and reality", and so the dynamic character of the sacred is highlighted: through it the whole world is to be transformed into the worship and adoration of God, but this will be fully realized only at the end of time.[43] Human existence in this world is structured by space and time, and so are prayer and

[43] J. Ratzinger, *The Spirit of the Liturgy*, trans. J. Saward (San Francisco: Ignatius Press, 2000), 54 (JRCW 11:31–32).

divine worship. Therefore the liturgy needs a place where it can be carried out as a "sacred action". In the words of Pope Benedict XVI's homily for the solemnity of Corpus Christi 2012:

> God . . . sent his Son into the world not to abolish, but to give fulfilment also to the sacred. At the height of this mission, at the Last Supper, Jesus instituted the Sacrament of his Body and his Blood, the Memorial of his Paschal Sacrifice. By so doing he replaced the ancient sacrifices with himself, but he did so in a rite which he commanded the Apostles to perpetuate, as a supreme sign of the true Sacred, which is he himself.[44]

[44] Benedict XVI, *Homily at the Holy Mass for the Solemnity of Corpus Christi* (June 7, 2012); the translation of the last phrase has been modified in light of the German version. The pope also noted the "educational function" of the sacred and warned that "its disappearance inevitably impoverishes culture and especially the formation of the new generations. If, for example, in the name of a faith that is secularized and no longer in need of sacred signs, these *Corpus Christi* processions through the city were to be abolished, the spiritual profile of Rome would be 'flattened out', and our personal and community awareness would be weakened. Or let us think of a mother or father who in the name of a desacralized faith, deprived their children of all religious rituals: in reality they would end by giving a free hand to the many substitutes that exist in the consumer society, to other rites and other signs that could more easily become idols."

EXCURSUS

Liturgy in the Mass Media

Broadcasting liturgical celebrations, especially Holy Mass, on television and other visual media is a common phenomenon today. Their usefulness is generally accepted for three main reasons:[45]

First, telecast Masses sustain the presence of the Church in the public sphere, allowing a wide diffusion for her central and most significant act of divine worship.

Secondly, telecast Masses provide a service for those who are not able to take part physically at a liturgical celebration (those who are hospitalized, homebound, or imprisoned). While following a Mass on TV never substitutes for actual participation in a worshipping assembly, it can nonetheless provide spiritual fruits, healing, and comfort.

Thirdly, broadcasts of liturgical celebrations in the mass media can be a useful tool for evangelization and catechesis. They can reach non-practicing Catholics and allow people of any creed or affiliation a means of encountering the Church and of learning about the faith.

Given these obvious advantages of telecast liturgies, it comes as no surprise that they were welcomed by the Church's hierarchy when the possibility arose. Pope Pius XII highly praised the initiative to broadcast for the first time

[45] Cf. B. Seveso, "La trasmissione televisiva della messa nelle valutazioni del magistero ecclesiastico", *Rivista liturgica* 84 (1997): 89–109, at 89–91.

Mass on Christmas Day 1948 from Notre Dame Cathedral in Paris.[46]

In subsequent years, most local episcopates showed themselves favorable to the introduction of televised Masses, with the notable exception of Austria. However, the new opportunities also raised concerns that led two Catholic thinkers from different perspectives, Karl Rahner and Josef Pieper, to reject them outright in 1953.[47] The all-pervading presence of the mass media in our world would simply not allow for such a categorical refusal today. Nonetheless, the objections raised by Rahner and Pieper can help us to establish criteria that should be followed for the broadcast of liturgical celebrations.

As Pieper observed, a sacred action, such as the liturgy, requires a threshold or even barrier that clearly distinguishes it from the sphere of the quotidian (the street and the marketplace). This threshold is mitigated, removed, or simply ignored by a telecast Mass. The sacred liturgy is of course the Church's solemn *public* worship and thus never has a purely private character. However, as the celebration of the mystery of faith, the liturgy has always required a certain *disciplina arcani* that does not allow for the extreme kind of publicity that is characteristic of contemporary mass media. The Liturgy of the Eucharist in particular is for the "initiated", and for this reason in many Christian rites the Liturgy of the Word was and is concluded with the dismissal

[46] Pius XII, *Discours aux fidèles, retransmis pour la première fois par la télévision française* (April 17, 1949).

[47] K. Rahner, "Die Messe und das Fernsehen", *Orientierung* 17 (1953): 179–83; J. Pieper, "Zur Fernseh-Übertragung der Heiligen Messe (1953)", in Pieper, *Werke*, vol. 7, *Religionsphilosophische Schriften*, ed. B. Wald (Hamburg: Felix Meiner, 2000), 487–90.

of catechumens, penitents, and other groups who cannot be admitted to this most sacred part of the rite.[48]

Moreover, each liturgical celebration is a unique event in time. In a mass culture that is characterized by technical reproduction, this uniqueness is not respected. The broadcast of the papal Mass on Easter Day, for instance, can be watched again and again outside its proper setting in the Church's liturgical year. The German cultural critic Walter Benjamin's reflections on the work of art in the age of mechanical reproduction also apply, *mutatis mutandis*, to the sacred liturgy. In particular, Benjamin speaks of the loss of the "aura" a work of art suffers when it is reproduced by merely technical means. Such aura is bound to the "here and now", the unique presence in space and time, which is lacking in technical reproduction.[49]

Televised Masses naturally do not allow for sacramental participation in the Holy Eucharist, but they also raise the question of how they can meet the demand for the faithful's "full, conscious, and active participation"[50] at all. The medium of television lacks physical interaction and necessarily leads people to a more passive role as spectators. The challenge for any liturgical broadcast is to engage the viewers

[48] Cf. C. Bell, *Ritual: Perspectives and Dimensions* (New York: Oxford University Press, 1997), 242–51; this section on "Media and Message" also gives a brief summary of the discussion preceding the coronation of Queen Elizabeth II on June 2, 1953, whether or not the event should be televised. A favorable decision was reached, with the exception of the act of anointing the monarch's forehead, the most sacred part of the rite, which was concealed from the cameras.

[49] W. Benjamin, "Das Kunstwerk im Zeitalter seiner technischen Reproduzierbarkeit (Dritte Fassung)", in Benjamin, *Gesammelte Schriften*, vol. 1. *Werkausgabe*, vol. 2, ed. R. Tiedemann and H. Schweppenhäuser (Frankfurt am Main: Suhrkamp, 1980), 471–508, esp. 475–78.

[50] *Sacrosanctum Concilium*, no. 14.

by uniting them spiritually with the prayers and chants, by making them listen attentively to the word of God, and by moving them to sentiments of penance, praise, thanksgiving, and adoration. In short, televised liturgies, while not allowing viewers to participate externally, should aim at involving them internally, so that they can join the actual liturgical assembly in the offering of Christ in the Holy Sacrifice.

The Second Vatican Council's Constitution on the Sacred Liturgy provides some general principles on the subject: "Transmissions of the sacred rites by radio and television shall be done with discretion and dignity, under the leadership and direction of a suitable person appointed for this office by the bishops. This is especially important when the service to be broadcast is the Mass."[51]

Likewise, the Sacred Congregation for the Sacraments and Divine Worship, in its Instruction *Inaestimabile Donum* of 1980, notes: "Particular vigilance and special care are recommended with regard to Masses transmitted by the audiovisual media. Given their very wide diffusion, their celebration must be of exemplary quality."[52]

Apart from this brief paragraph, the Congregation has not formulated a position on the question. In fact, it is in the competence of the Local Ordinary to regulate the television broadcast of liturgical celebrations, and several conferences of bishops have published guidelines on the matter, among them Germany and the United States of America.[53] Such

[51] Ibid., no. 20.

[52] Sacred Congregation for the Sacraments and Divine Worship, Instruction *Inaestimabile Donum* concerning Worship of the Eucharistic Mystery (April 17, 1980), 19.

[53] Sekretariat der Deutschen Bischofskonferenz, *Gottesdienst-Übertragungen in Hörfunk und Fernsehen: Leitlinien und Empfehlungen 2002*, 2nd ed., 2007 (revised and extended version of the guidelines originally published in 1989)

guidelines are highly desirable, because liturgists and communication specialists who work on the televising of liturgical celebrations, usually Sunday Mass, tend to encounter many difficulties. The medium itself imposes constraints, and the Church's control over the broadcasting process is usually limited.

Among the guidelines that have been prepared by various bishops' conferences, the following points would seem to be the most pertinent ones:

1. The bishop of a diocese in which a televised Mass is produced has the responsibility to see that liturgical law is carefully observed, following the rubrics and the directives of the *Instructio Generalis Missalis Romani*. Given the potentially wide diffusion of a televised liturgical celebration, the bishop's vigilance is particularly important.

2. It is always desirable that the liturgy should be telecast "live", in real time, as it is celebrated. When this is not possible, it should preferably be recorded and shown on the same day. If there is no other way than prerecording the liturgy, it should be done as close as possible to the date of the broadcast, so that the integrity of the liturgical year may be kept.[54]

---

dbk.de/fileadmin/redaktion/veroeffentlichungen/arbeitshilfen/AH_169.pdf (accessed April 19, 2014); United States Conference of Catholic Bishops, *Guidelines for Televising the Liturgy*, 2014 (updated version of the guidelines issued in 1997) http://usccb.org/prayer-and-worship/the-mass/frequently-asked-questions/guidelines-for-televising-the-liturgy.cfm (accessed July 2, 2015).

[54] It is particularly out of keeping with the rhythm of liturgical time to record an Easter Sunday Mass in Lent, as has apparently been the regular practice in the Diocese of Albany, New York. See the diocesan "Office of Prayer and Worship Newsletter", vol. 14, no. 1, January-February 2012, http://www.rcda.org/Offices/prayer_and_worship/Newsletters/2012/jan-feb%202012.pdf. The recordings are available on the diocese's YouTube channel

3. The problem of time constraints needs to be considered carefully and in advance of the production. Public television usually requires a particular time frame that can affect the liturgical celebration in negative ways. However, the liturgical celebration should not be rushed, nor should elements that are integral to it be omitted.[55] Precise planning can help to meet the requirements of TV producers while respecting the integrity of the liturgy.

4. The participants in the celebration need to be particularly prepared. Above all, the celebrant priest and the ministers will need to pay the utmost attention to their *ars celebrandi*, because they will be recorded by television cameras, which can be merciless in exposing human idiosyncrasies. If a Mass is transmitted from a specific setting, such as a smaller chapel, the faithful who take part in it also need to be made aware that the way they pray, sing, and comport themselves will contribute to the overall impression of the broadcast.

5. Broadcasting a liturgical celebration presents a particular challenge to those who record and produce it. In particular, a televised Mass calls for an intelligent direction of the camera. Television by its very nature wants a movement of images, and the dynamism of the medium has increased dramatically in recent years. There are moments in liturgical celebrations that will lend themselves to this aesthetic of movement, such as the entrance procession

---

http://www.youtube.com/user/DioceseOfAlbany?feature=watch (both accessed August 24, 2013).

[55] To cite just one example: at the Ash Wednesday Mass in Munich Cathedral on February 22, 2012, which was broadcast by Bavarian State Television (*Bayerischer Rundfunk*), the distribution of the ashes had to be interrupted to let the celebration continue within its given time frame. As a result, probably more than one hundred people in the nave did not receive the ashes at the proper moment.

or the Gospel procession, not to mention particular rites during the liturgical year that have an immediate appeal to the viewer, but as a whole the Mass is more static than a television producer would probably wish for. The broadcast will need to be made more appealing to viewers; a historical church, for instance, with a rich artistic decoration can help in this regard: at particular moments, showing an image that is related to a biblical reading or to a liturgical prayer can be a visual translation of the word that is spoken. At the same time, the camera should exercise discretion in certain moments of the celebration; for instance, it should avoid showing the faces of people when they receive Holy Communion in order to protect the sacred and intimate character of the act.

6. The commentary on the liturgical celebration also calls for careful attention. In general, a commentator should be well prepared and have a good understanding of the rites and ceremonies. It will help if a journalist is assisted by an ecclesiastic in this task. Obviously, their contribution is essential if a liturgy is televised that is not celebrated in the national language. The commentary should, however, be discreet and not overburdening. There is a tendency among commentators to fill moments that are considered uninteresting for the viewer. However, sacred silence is part of the liturgy, and this should be respected in a television broadcast. Moreover, commentary should not overlay the music that is an integral part of the liturgical celebration. Technical means, such as subtitles, can provide the text of a chant to facilitate its understanding on the part of the viewers.

This list of guidelines is not meant to be complete, and further points will no doubt emerge from the concrete experience of those involved in broadcasting liturgical celebrations. The medium itself imposes demands that are not always easy to meet. However, it is of the utmost importance to maintain the spirit of the liturgy, in complete harmony with the mind of the Church, and, in close collaboration with media professionals, to find the best way possible to communicate the sacredness of the liturgical action to the viewers in front of the screen.

1. Massimiliano Fuksas, San Paolo, Foligno, Italy, credit Moreno Maggi

2. Church of the Gesù, Rome, Italy, credit Alessio Damato, wikimedia.com

3. Massimiliano Fuksas, San Paolo, Foligno, Italy, credit sacredarchitecture.org

4. Mario Botta, Evry Cathedral, France, credit flickr user nicolasnova

5. Mario Botta, Cymbalista synagogue and heritage center, Tel Aviv, Israel, credit Michael Jacobson, wikimedia.com

6. Rafael Moneo, Los Angeles Cathedral, California, credit David Leigh Ellis, wikimedia.com

7. & 8. Duncan Stroik, Thomas Aquinas College Chapel, Santa Paula, California, credit schafphoto

9. Thomas Gordon Smith, Seminary Chapel,
Denton, Nebraska, credit Alex Begin

10. Thomas Gordon Smith, Seminary Chapel,
Denton, Nebraska, credit Thomas D. Stroka

III

Sacred Architecture: Crisis and Renewal

In the preceding chapter, the understanding of the sacred in Christianity was reformulated in close relation with the liturgy, which is the exercise of the priestly office of Jesus Christ in his Mystical Body, the Church. This chapter will explore the question of how this renewed conception of the sacred can be translated into the design and construction of buildings dedicated to the liturgy. The history of church architecture shows a great richness and variety in the attempts of achieving this translation. It is not my aim to pursue this history here.[1] Rather, I propose to look at questions that have been raised by contemporary church buildings, questions that ultimately concern the visible expression of the sacred. By way of introduction, I should like to discuss the views of two well-known architects who have designed important churches in recent years.

Massimiliano Fuksas: There Is No "Sacred Architecture"

The internationally renowned Italian architect Massimiliano Fuksas in collaboration with his wife, Doriana Mandrelli,

[1] See, for instance, A. Doig, *Liturgy and Architecture: From the Early Church to the Middle Ages*, Liturgy, Worship and Society (Farnham and Burlington, Vt.: Ashgate, 2008), and the concise introduction by D. R. McNamara, *How*

completed in 2009 the church of San Paolo in Foligno, Umbria. This church is one of the "pilot projects" (*progetti pilota*) of the Italian Bishops' Conference and has attracted much attention—and controversy.

In a long interview given in April 2009, Fuksas reflects on the ideas that guided him in this project.[2] As he makes clear at the beginning of the conversation, he does not believe "that you can do sacred architecture"; what is possible is "architecture that tends to spirituality".[3] Such spirituality is diffusely articulated, above all with reference to light, not only as an architectural element but also as a philosophical principle.

For Fuksas, the relationship of a building with its exterior environment is of key importance. The particular character of a church is manifest in the fact that it stands out. Fuksas observes that most contemporary constructions, either for housing or other functional purposes, create urban spaces that lack a center or point of reference. With his church in Foligno, the architect wants to "return to a structure that is no longer horizontal", a development he associates with the Second Vatican Council, and he sees in his accent on the height of the building a reference to Gothic architecture. In the church at Foligno, this vertical dimension is in fact a striking feature that is realized by its sheer height (*Illustration 1*).[4]

---

to Read Churches: A Crash Course in Ecclesiastical Architecture (Lewes: Rizzoli, 2011).

[2] P. Ansideri, *La Bottega dell'Architetto: Conversazione con Massimiliano Fuksas sulla chiesa di Foligno . . . ed altro* (Rome, April 17, 2009) http://www.oicosriflessioni.it/wp-content/uploads/2011/07/corretto-Paolo-05-10-11-intervista-fuksas.pdf (accessed April 25, 2013), 1.

[3] "La prima cosa da dire è che io non credo si possa fare architettura sacra. Si può fare architettura che tende alla spiritualità. L'architettura sacra o l'architettura profana non vogliono dire nulla": ibid.

[4] See ibid.

Special attention is given to the façade and the entrance to the church. Fuksas rejects the "church of the Counter-Reformation", which he sees exemplified in the Church of the *Gesù* in Rome (consecrated in 1584): "You enter after being attracted by a great staircase, a great façade, by the dynamism, by the majesty of the façade and by [its] great power. You enter because it is an act of faith. Once you enter inside, you understand that this faith is something extremely complex" (*Illustration 2*).[5] Fuksas' own concept of the façade could not be more different: in extreme abstraction, it presents itself as one side of the cube that is the shape of the building, in plain concrete and without any ornamentation or prominent Christian symbolism. The entrance to the church, which is marked by a front of glass doors and windows on the ground floor and includes a relatively small cross, is reached by means of a large ramp (*Illustration 3*).

Inside the church, the actual liturgical space makes a banal and, in a strange way, dated expression. On visiting the church in Foligno in 2010, I was reminded of churches of the 1970s that have aged badly, although this church had been completed only one year before. Of note are also the attempts (presumably of the parish community) to make the church a "home" to regular worshippers by including a traditional large crucifix, a historical tabernacle, and a Baroque statue of the Blessed Virgin Mary.

The rejection of the idea that a church should distinguish itself as a Christian sacred building in its architectural forms is not original to Fuksas, but it is typical of the modernist movement as such. Commenting on his famous chapel

[5] "Io non sono per la chiesa controriformista, come la chiesa del Gesù, come la chiesa del Vignola, che tu entri dopo essere stato attratto da una grande scalinata, da una grande facciata, dalla dinamicità, dalla possanza della facciata e dal grande potere. Tu entri perché è un atto di fede. Entrato dentro capisci che questa fede è qualche cosa di estremamente complesso": ibid., 2.

of Notre Dame du Haut at Ronchamp (1955), Le Corbusier explained that "the requirements of religion" had little impact on the design; the form was rather intended to stir "the psychophysiology of the feelings".[6] Likewise Mies van der Rohe, when he designed the chapel at the Illinois Institute of Technology (1952), is said to have been "interested not in the specific solution for the church . . . but in the universal form; an architecture which could accommodate any function".[7]

More recently, when Santiago Calatrava presented his design for the Cathedral of Christ the Light in Oakland, California, which originally won the commission but was then not executed, he stated his ambition to give the building "a universal character independent of the Catholic Church", because of the many different cultures in the city.[8] The relationship between faith and culture that is implicit in such statements calls, at the very least, for some clarification.

Mario Botta: Architecture in Itself a Sacred Work

The Swiss-Italian architect Mario Botta is distinguished not only by the number of significant churches he has designed, such as the Cathedral of the Resurrection at Evry near Paris (dedicated in 1995) and the Church of the Holy Face in Turin (2006), but also by his theoretical reflections on the subject of sacred architecture.

[6] Le Corbusier, *Œuvre complète*, vol. 5: *1946–52*, ed. W. Boesiger (Basel: Birkhäuser, 2006), 72.

[7] E. Heathcote and I. Spens, *Church Builders* (Chichester: Academy Editions, 1997), 56.

[8] Z. Sardar, "Cathedral Dreams", *San Francisco Chronicle Magazine*, February 18, 2001, http://sfgate.com/bayarea/article/CATHEDRAL-DREAMS-Celebrated-for-skeletal-2950579.php (accessed July 2, 2015).

In a lecture given at Zurich a few years ago, Botta observes that buildings have the capacity of communicating "values" that transcend their proper function. One such value is the sacred, which he describes as the realization of a connection that leads us beyond the technical or functional aspects of a building and allows us to recall an experience of a reality that transcends what is immediately perceptible to the senses.[9] Note that the sacred *recalls* this experience: for Botta, the idea of the sacred is linked with a particular history or memory.

It would appear that this memory is constituted in the act of building itself, which he elsewhere defines as a "sacred act": "it is an action that transforms a condition of nature into a condition of culture; the story of architecture is the story of these transformations."[10] Botta appears convinced, therefore, that *any* architecture carries within itself the idea of the sacred, in that it is an expression of human work. The first step of "making architecture" begins by putting a stone on the ground, and this action in itself has a sacred meaning, because it transforms a condition that is not controlled by human activity, at least not exclusively, into a living space formed by man. The second step consists in marking a boundary, without which no architecture exists.

[9] M. Botta, "Räume des Übergangs", in M. Botta, G. Böhm, P. Böhm, R. Moneo, *Sakralität und Aura in der Architektur*, Architekturvorträge der ETH Zürich (Zürich: GTA Verlag, 2010), 10–51, at 13: "Eine erste Betrachtung gilt dem Phänomen des Sakralen: Es ist ein Phänomen der Umsetzung einer Spannung, einer Verbindung, die uns über die Fakten, die technischen Nutzungsfunktionen hinausführt und uns dazu bringt, etwas *wiederzuerleben*, das eine vordergründige Wahrnehmung übersteigt" (emphasis mine).

[10] "Costruire è di per sé un atto sacro, è una azione che trasforma una condizione di natura in una condizione di cultura; la storia dell'architettura è la storia di queste trasformazioni": M. Botta, "Lo spazio del sacro" in *Architetture del sacro: Preghiere di pietra*, ed. G. Cappellato (Bologna: Editrice Compositori, 2005), 3–5, at 3. Cf. Botta, "Räume des Übergangs", 13–14.

Thus an "interior and therefore sacred" realm or state is separated from the exterior.[11]

This refers to the construction not only of a church (or synagogue or mosque) but of any edifice. A building is considered an expression of the human labor that created it, with all its joys and efforts, and so communicates sentiments and aspirations that, according to Botta, "belong to the spiritual sphere". The building thus holds a sacred potential as a memorial to the transforming force of human work.[12] Botta claims that the history of architecture in the Western Christian tradition is largely one of church architecture. By comparison, he regards the impact of civil and military architecture before the twentieth century as marginal. An architectural historian may well dispute this statement, but this is not our concern here.

This extension of the category of the sacred to architecture as such raises the question of what, if anything at all, is

[11] "Sobald man auf dem Boden eine Perimeterlinie einzeichnet, trennt man einen inneren, *also sakralen* Zustand vom äusseren". Botta, "Räume des Übergangs", 14 (emphasis mine).

[12] "Io credo che l'architettura porti con sé l'idea del sacro, nel senso che è espressione del lavoro dell'uomo. L'architettura non è solo un'organizzazione materiale; anche la più povera delle capanne ha una sua storia, una sua dignità, una sua etica che testimonia di un vissuto, di una memoria, parla delle più segrete aspirazioni dell'uomo. L'architettura è una disciplina dove—più che in altri settori—la memoria gioca un ruolo fondamentale; dopo anni di lavoro mi sembra di capire come il territorio su cui opera l'architetto si configuri sempre più come 'spazio della memoria'; il territorio fisico parla di una storia geologica, antropologica, ma anche di una memoria più umile legata al lavoro dell'uomo. Ecco che allora, da questo punto di vista, l'architettura porta con sé un potenziale di sacro perché testimonia una saggezza 'del fare' con gioie e fatiche che trasmettono sentimenti ed emozioni che appartengono alla sfera spirituale. Di fronte ad una casa o ad una chiesa proviamo un'emozione che non è solo data dal fatto costruttivo in sé ma dai significati simbolici e metaforici": C. Donati, "A colloquio con Mario Botta: le nuove forme della memoria", *Costruire in Laterizio* 72 (November/December 1999): 40–44, at 41.

added to this in the building of a church. Botta introduces the aspect of durability or solidity, which he defines as "creating an artefact (*manufatto*) as a physical presence between earth and heaven".[13] This would seem to be connected with Botta's conviction that nature should be integrated into architecture and vice versa, because they are complementing each other—an idea he realized, for instance, in his cathedral of Evry in France, where a crown of trees is set on top of the cylindrical structure (*Illustration 4*).[14]

The noted architect describes a church as "an elementary space for the assembly, where for the faithful the original event of the Christian sacrifice is repeated".[15] This description can serve as a starting point for a conversation on the historically formed understanding of church building. Botta also speaks of the necessity not to subject this space to changing fashions and mentions as his ideal style the Romanesque because of the austerity of its forms. Still, with the extension of the sacred to all architecture, it remains unclear what distinguishes a building dedicated to divine worship from any other construction.

It will be instructive also to consider Botta's Cymbalista Synagogue and Jewish Heritage Centre in Tel Aviv. The University of Tel Aviv, anxious to respect the secular tradition of the city as well, decided that the religious building

[13] "Per esempio, costruire una chiesa vuole anche dire confrontarsi con il tema della durata, della solidità, vuol dire creare un manufatto come presenza fisica fra terra e cielo": ibid.

[14] The "sliced cylinder" is a characteristic of Botta's ecclesiastical buildings and also features in his church of San Giovanni Battista, Mogno (1986–1996), and in his chapel of Santa Maria degli Angeli, Monte Tamaro (1990–1996), both in the Swiss Alps.

[15] "La chiesa è comunque uno spazio assembleare elementare dove per il fedele si ripete l'evento originale del sacrificio cristiano": Donati, "A colloquio", 41.

should not dominate the structure and therefore asked the architect to construct a cultural center next to it. The architect interpreted this request by making both edifices, the sacred and the secular, identical in form and dimensions, in the materials and in the light design (*Illustration 5*). In his comments on this project, Botta notes that he deliberately went against the hailed principle of modern architecture that form should follow function. Here, the same form serves two functions, which are quite separate from each other.[16]

The reflections of both Fuksas and Botta—albeit in different ways—lack appreciation for the characteristics of the sacred in Christianity and hence for the *function* (in a profound sense) of a church, the celebration of the liturgy. The theological positions discussed in the previous chapter may not have had a direct impact on contemporary architects, many of whom probably approach a church like any other commission they receive. Nonetheless, ideas have consequences, and the movement of desacralization within Christianity certainly had its effect on church building. It would seem evident to me that these theological currents have contributed to a type of building that does not adequately express the sacred. This weakness or, in some cases, failure is not simply a question of architectural styles but is rather a question of the theoretical presuppositions that have gone into these projects, even if they are not always articulated. In the following sections I shall attempt to sketch the essential requirements Catholic theology and practice make on the building of a church.

[16] See Botta, "Räume des Übergangs", 36–39.

Theological Foundations of Church Architecture

The sacred building of Christianity is different from the temple of classical antiquity, where the *cella*, or inner chamber, containing the cult image or statue was considered the dwelling place of the divinity. It was most likely in reference to this idea that the apostle Saint Paul is reported to have told the Athenians, "The God who made the world and everything in it, being Lord of heaven and earth, does not live in shrines made by man" (Acts 17:24).

There is a closer analogy with the places where God revealed his presence to the people of Israel: the Tent of Meeting in the desert and the Temple of Jerusalem. Among the rich testimonies in the Pentateuch on the Tent, there is the passage where the Lord himself assures Moses in Exodus 25:22: "There I will meet with you, and from above the mercy seat, from between the two cherubim that are on the ark of the covenant, I will speak with you of all that I wil give you in commandment for the Sons of Israel". The Book of Exodus also describes the descent of God's glory (40:34): "Then the cloud covered the tent of meeting, and the glory of the LORD filled the tabernacle."

Likewise, when God appeared to Solomon, after the building of the Temple of Jerusalem, he declared: "I have consecrated this house which you have built, and put my name there for ever; my eyes and my heart will be there for all time" (1 Kings 9:3). Thus the presence of the transcendent God in the Holy of Holies of the Temple, which rabbinic literature called *shekinah*, became the focus of Jewish prayer, even in the Diaspora and after (1 Kings 8:38, 44, 48; Dan 6:10).

However, the idea of a quasi-physical dwelling place of God

was already questioned by Solomon himself, just after his magnificent Temple had been completed: "But will God indeed dwell on the earth? Behold, heaven and the highest heaven cannot contain you; how much less this house which I have built!" (1 Kings 8:27). On this point the Book of Isaiah is emphatic: "The whole earth is full of his glory" (Is 6:3; cf. Jer 23:24; Ps 139:1–18; Wis 1:7)—a text that would later be included in the *Sanctus* of the Eucharistic liturgy.[17]

This line of thought is carried farther in the New Testament. During his encounter with the Samaritan woman at Jacob's well as related in Saint John's Gospel, Jesus declares: "The hour is coming, and now is, when the true worshipers will worship the Father in spirit and truth, for such the Father seeks to worship him" (Jn 4:23). As so often in the Fourth Gospel, there are various layers of meaning here: first, and most literally, the worship inaugurated by Christ is contrasted with Jewish and Samaritan worship, because it is "in spirit", that is, not confined to a single sanctuary, like the Temple of Jerusalem for the Jews or Mount Gerizim for the Samaritans. This does not mean, however, that there should be no places and buildings for worship under the New Covenant. The English theologian, Oratorian, and cardinal, John Henry Newman (1801–1890), put this well when he said: "The glory of the Gospel is not the *abolition* of rites, but their *dissemination*; not their absence, but their living and efficacious presence through the grace of Christ."[18] The point is not that there should not be any place built to God's honor but, rather, that there should be many of them.

In his book on the *Spirit of the Liturgy*, Joseph Ratzinger

[17] Cf. V. Gatti, *Liturgia e arte: I luoghi della celebrazione* (Bologna: EDB, 2001), 49–50 and 67–68.

[18] J. H. Newman, *Parochial and Plain Sermons* VI, 19: "The Gospel Palaces" (San Francisco: Ignatius Press, 1997), 1354–60, at 1355.

identifies universality as an essential feature of Christian worship and links Christ's announcement of adoration "in spirit and truth", which is not tied to a single place, to his prophetic word about the destruction and rebuilding of the temple. During the trial before the high priest, this word was taken to refer to the Temple of Jerusalem (Mt 26:61). Ratzinger recalls the clarification of the Evangelist John in his account of the cleansing of the Temple, declaring that Jesus "spoke of the temple of his body" (Jn 2:21), and comments:

> Jesus does not say that *he* will demolish the Temple—that version was the false witness borne against him. But he does prophesy that his accusers will do exactly that. This is a prophecy of the Cross: he shows that the destruction of his earthly body will be at the same time the end of the Temple. With his Resurrection the new Temple will begin: the living body of Jesus Christ, which will now stand in the sight of God and be the place of all worship. Into this body he incorporates men. It is the tabernacle that no human hands have made, the place of true worship of God, which casts out the shadow and replaces it with reality.[19]

Thus Christ's words are to be understood as a prophecy of the Cross and of the Resurrection. The new Temple, the new Tent not made by human hands, is Christ's Body, in both its ecclesiological and its Eucharistic dimension. That is, the place of true worship is the Church, the Mystical Body of Christ, into which the faithful are incorporated. Here worship "in spirit and in truth" is offered to the eternal Father. As is clear from the Fourth Gospel, "spirit" and "truth" are not to be understood as abstract philosophical concepts, but in a christological sense, indicating those divine

[19] J. Ratzinger, *The Spirit of the Liturgy*, trans. J. Saward (San Francisco: Ignatius Press, 2000), 43 (JRCW 11:25).

realities that make present him who revealed himself as "the truth" (Jn 14:6) and promised to send his Spirit.[20]

Thus the "place" of Christian worship is *Christus totus*, Christ the Head and the baptized as the members of his Mystical Body. The faithful who are gathered in one place for divine worship are the "living stones", joined to build "a spiritual house, to be a holy priesthood, to offer spiritual sacrifices acceptable to God through Jesus Christ" (1 Pet 2:5). It is significant that the word used in the biblical tradition to denote the assembly of worship, "church" (*qahal*, *ekklēsia*), came to indicate the very place in which this worship would take place.[21] By virtue of the sacrament of baptism, the faithful share in the priesthood of Christ, though not in the ministerial priesthood. They participate in the sacramental offering of Christ's sacrifice to the Father in the Holy Spirit, as expressed in the liturgical prayers of offering that use the first person plural, such as the Roman Canon of the Mass: "we, your servants and your holy people, offer to your glorious majesty".[22]

Thus the Christian liturgy assigns to the people a much more important role than did pagan worship in antiquity, when they did not directly participate in the act of offering. This fundamental antithesis is manifest in different concep-

[20] Cf. J. Ratzinger, "The Theology of the Liturgy", a lecture delivered during the Journées Liturgiques de Fontgombault, July 22–24 2001, in JRCW 11:541–57, at 553.

[21] Cf. Augustine, *Ep. 190 ad Optatum*, 19: Corpus Scriptorum Ecclesiasticorum Latinorum 57,154: "Sicut ergo appellamus ecclesiam basilicam, qua continetur populus, qui vere appellatur ecclesia, ut nomine ecclesiae, id est, populi, qui continetur, significemus locum, qui continet, ita, quod animae corporibus continentur, intellegi corpora filiorum per nominatas animas possunt."

[22] Cf. Pius XII, Encyclical on the Sacred Liturgy *Mediator Dei* (November 20, 1947), nos. 85–87; Second Vatican Council, Constitution on the Sacred Liturgy *Sacrosanctum Concilium* (December 4, 1963), no. 48.

tions of sacred architecture. The classical temple has an "extroverted" character: its significant architectural and artistic elements, such as columns, friezes, and sculptures, are placed on the outside of the building. This external magnificence and splendor was designed for the worshippers who remained outside the inner sanctum. Christians, however, as soon as they were able to develop a monumental architecture, adopted the form of the basilica, which provided a large interior space where the faithful could gather for worship. Churches thus have an "introverted" character, because precious materials and decorative elements are above all found inside the building. In the early Christian basilicas, a striking contrast can often been observed between the plain exterior and the elaborate and (depending on the available means) sumptuous interior, especially the iconography. The arrangement of specific elements, such as altar, ambo, seats for the clergy, and screens, soon developed in distinct ways in various parts of the Christian world. External aspects, above all the façade, received greater attention only later, when the public presence of Christianity was consolidated.

As Pope Benedict XVI notes in his Post-Synodal Apostolic Exhortation *Sacramentum Caritatis*, "the purpose of sacred architecture is to offer the Church a fitting space for the celebration of the mysteries of faith, especially the Eucharist. The very nature of a Christian church is defined by the liturgy."[23] The *Catechism of the Catholic Church* insists

[23] Cf. Benedict XVI, Post-Synodal Apostolic Exhortation *Sacramentum Caritatis* on the Eucharist as the Source and Summit of the Church's Life and Mission (February 22, 2007), no. 41. For the Ordinary Form of the Roman Rite, general indications in this regard are given in *The Roman Missal: Renewed by Decree of the Most Holy Second Ecumenical Council of the Vatican, Promulgated by Authority of Pope Paul VI and Revised at the Direction of Pope John Paul II*, English translation according to the third typical edition (London: Catholic

that a church is not simply a "gathering place" but is "the dwelling of God with men reconciled and united in Christ" and is therefore rightly called "house of God".[24]

Architects of the Sacred

A Catholic understanding of the church as a sacred building is both rich and complex. Does this mean that the architects embarking on such a project will have to be theologians in their own right? Not necessarily. What is required, however, is the willingness to enter into a conversation with their clients in order to arrive at a full, sacramental understanding of the church building. This is a challenge not only for architects but also for the ecclesiastical patrons. On reading the published version of a lecture by Rafael Moneo, I was struck by his comments on one of two essential requirements he followed in his design of the Los Angeles Cathedral, completed in 2002 (*Illustration 6*), namely, "the orientation of the apse, which according to ecclesiastic tradition had to face Rome in recognition of the importance of ecumenism for the Catholic congregation".[25] Such a comment on the sacred direction of church buildings betrays above all a failure of theological and liturgical consultancy in the planning of a major ecclesiastical

---

Truth Society, 2011), *General Instruction of the Roman Missal*, chap. 5: "The Arrangement and Ornamentation of the Churches for the Celebration of the Eucharist", nos. 288–318.

[24] *Catechism of the Catholic Church*, 2nd ed. (Washington, D.C.: United States Catholic Conference, 2000), no. 1180, cf. nos. 1179–86.

[25] R. Moneo, "Cathedral of Our Lady of the Angels Los Angeles, CA, 1996–2002", in M. Botta, G. Böhm, P. Böhm, R. Moneo, *Sakralität und Aura in der Architektur*, Architekturvorträge der ETH Zürich (Zürich: GTA Verlag, 2010), 84–105, at 92.

edifice.[26] The lack of input on the part of the Church is a lost opportunity, as many architects, including those best known internationally, are still keen on building churches, as they seem to realize that here they have the chance to leave a monument of greater and more lasting significance. As Massimiliano Fuksas said in the interview cited earlier: "But a church is something you must do."[27]

In the last decade or so, the new classical movement has gained experience and maturity in the field of sacred architecture.[28] Two well-known examples, Thomas Aquinas College Chapel in Santa Paula, California, and Our Lady of Guadalupe Seminary Chapel in Denton, Nebraska, were designed by leading representatives of the University of Notre Dame's School of Architecture. While this school is committed to a classical style of building, there is a notable difference between Duncan Stroik's elaborate use of elements from the Italian Renaissance and the colonial Spanish Baroque period at Thomas Aquinas College (*Illustrations 7 and 8*), and Thomas Gordon Smith's restrained Romanesque style in accordance with the wishes of his client, the Fraternity of Saint Peter in Denton (*Illustrations 9 and 10*). From a ritual perspective, this continuity of form is highly significant. As Roy Rappaport has observed, the mere existence of an ancient cathedral not only speaks of "the endurance of a liturgical order and its relationship to a place and a group" but "demonstrates it". Likewise, a new building modelled on a traditional form "substantiates the continuing vitality,

[26] I have treated the topic at some length in my *Turning Towards the Lord: Orientation in Liturgical Prayer*, 2nd ed. (San Francisco: Ignatius Press, 2009).

[27] "Però una chiesa è una cosa che devi fare:" Ansideri, *La Bottega dell'Architetto: Conversazione con Massimiliano Fuksas*, 6.

[28] D. R. McNamara, "A Decade of New Classicism: The Flowering of Traditional Church Architecture", *Sacred Architecture* 21 (2012): 18–24.

propriety or correctness of that form".[29] We should not be afraid of imitation, because in this process something new is created, as the historical periods of the Renaissance or of Classicism show us. It is my conviction that this is our best option to renew sacred architecture today. At the same time, it should be noted that such a renewal is not linked to one particular style. It would be mistaken to conclude that *only* a stark and simple style or *only* an ornate and exuberant one is capable of expressing the sacred. However, an architecture that is not ready, or even refuses, to let itself be formed by the Church's liturgy does not work as a church building, as the historical styles of Christianity do.

To conclude this chapter, I should like to propose four general principles of sacred architecture. These are suggestions made for the purpose of discussion; they are not meant to be exhaustive or definitive.[30]

The first principle is *verticality*: a church needs to have a clearly expressed vertical dimension that goes beyond the functional demands of the building. It is not just by accident that historical churches are usually marked by their height. The vertical slant communicates a sense of God's transcendence and leads the worshipper to "seek the things that are above, where Christ is, seated at the right hand of God" (Col 3:1).

The second principle is *orientation*: a church should have a clear sense of directionality. When the Constantinian settlement in the early fourth century permitted the development

[29] R. A. Rappaport, *Ritual and Religion in the Making of Humanity*, Cambridge Studies in Social and Cultural Anthropology (Cambridge: Cambridge University Press, 1999), 144.

[30] See also the collection of essays by D. G. Stroik, *The Church Building as a Sacred Place: Beauty, Transcendence, and the Eternal* (Chicago: Hillenbrand Books, 2012). The author, who is both a practitioner and an academic teacher, presents general principles as well as concrete advice.

of a monumental Christian architecture, the type of building that was chosen throughout the Roman Empire was the basilica. While allowing variation in the arrangement of architectural elements, the basic structure of the basilica, with its long rectangular nave ending in a semicircular apse, was considered singularly suitable for the essential demands of Christian worship and became normative in the Western tradition. The ideal of the Christian church is not a circular building with altar, ambo, and sedilia in the center; it is not mere accident that samples of this type are rarely found before the second half of the twentieth century. Historical examples of central-plan churches are usually connected with a specific liturgical use, such as a *martyrion* or *memoria* (memorial buildings on a venerated tomb or other sacred place) and a baptistery. The clear directionality of the basilica layout expresses the worshipping community's actions of praying and offering to the Lord. The orientation of liturgical space, combined with the first principle of verticality, reaches beyond the visible altar toward eschatological fulfillment, which is anticipated in the celebration of the Holy Eucharist as a participation in the heavenly liturgy and a pledge of future glory in the presence of the living God. The cosmic symbolism of facing east also recalls that the liturgy "represents more than the coming together of a more or less large circle of people: the liturgy is celebrated in the expanse of the cosmos, encompassing creation and history at the same time" and so reminds us "that the Redeemer to whom we pray is also the Creator".[31]

The third principle is the need for *thresholds*. The work of Victor Turner, discussed in the first chapter of this book,

[31] Benedict XVI, "On the Inaugural Volume of My Collected Works", in JRCW 11:xi–xviii, at xvii.

has brought into relief the importance of liminality in ritual. The first such threshold is the entrance to the building, which should be not simply functional but monumental, part of a façade that marks the church as a building set apart. The *Catechism of the Catholic Church* notes the eschatological significance of the church entrance: "To enter into the house of God, we must cross a *threshold*, which symbolizes passing from the world wounded by sin to the world of the new Life to which all men are called."[32] Here is a limit or boundary that distinguishes the sacred building from the street or square where it stands but, at the same time, allows communication and passage between the two worlds. An outside precinct in the form of an atrium or a *sagrato*, as in Bernini's supreme model of the Vatican Basilica, is a particularly felicitous expression of this dynamic. The second important threshold concerns the sanctuary, which "should suitably be marked off from the body of the church either by its being somewhat elevated or by a particular structure and ornamentation".[33] A sanctuary raised by a few steps also allows better visibility and so gives a clearer sense of liturgical orientation. In historical churches, the sanctuary is framed by chancel screens or communion rails; thus a shrine is created within the church to highlight the altar, where the sacrifice of Christ is re-presented—a usage that should be revisited.

The fourth principle concerns the connection of sacred art and architecture. In his book *The Spirit of the Liturgy*, Joseph Ratzinger has formulated "fundamental principles of an art ordered to divine worship". The first of these principles is particularly relevant: "The complete absence of images

[32] *Catechism of the Catholic Church*, no. 1186.

[33] *General Instruction of the Roman Missal*, no. 295.

is incompatible with faith in the Incarnation of God. God has acted in history and entered into our sensible world, so that it may become transparent to him. Images of beauty, in which the mystery of the invisible God becomes visible, are an essential part of Christian worship. . . . Iconoclasm is not a Christian option."[34] In other words, Christian sacred art is essentially figurative. Such figurative art cannot be reduced to naturalism, and in fact the representation of the sacred demands an element of abstraction that will allow it to communicate the reality of the supernatural. This is evident not only from Byzantine iconography but also from the masters of the Western tradition, such as Fra Angelico.[35] Moreover, a church also contains space for symbolical and non-figurative expression, as found in the stained glass windows of Cistercian architecture. However, pure abstraction in the modern sense is not adequate, not for aesthetic but for theological reasons, and its presence in so many Catholic churches built more recently needs to be questioned.

Finally, the renewal of church architecture that is happening today needs to be supported by a more robust theological reflection on the sacred in Christianity, which will help architects to design apt and indeed beautiful buildings for the Catholic liturgy.

[34] Ratzinger, *Spirit of the Liturgy*, 131–32 (JRCW 11:81).

[35] See the somewhat overstated article by T. Verdon, "Anche il Beato Angelico era un astrattista", *L'Osservatore Romano* (January 12, 2008), 5.

IV

Sacred Art: The Search for Beauty

Any conversation about sacred art in the Catholic tradition has a firm point of reference in the seventh chapter of the Second Vatican Council's Constitution on the Sacred Liturgy, which is dedicated to "Sacred Art and Sacred Furnishings":

> Very rightly the fine arts are considered to rank among the noblest activities of man's genius, and this applies especially to religious art and to its highest achievement, which is sacred art. These arts, by their very nature, are oriented toward the infinite beauty of God which they attempt in some way to portray by the work of human hands; they achieve their purpose of redounding to God's praise and glory in proportion as they are directed the more exclusively to the single aim of turning men's minds devoutly toward God.[1]

This seminal paragraph, which will concern us throughout this chapter, introduces an important distinction between "religious art" and "sacred art". The theologian Enrico Cattaneo, commenting on this distinction in his historical study on liturgy and art, notes that religious art is characterized by the artist's personal approach to a religious theme. Because of this strongly subjective element, a work of religious art may not always be accessible to everyone.

[1] Second Vatican Council, Constitution on the Sacred Liturgy *Sacrosanctum Concilium* (December 4, 1963), no. 122.

By contrast, sacred art is born from the artist's engagement with and reflection upon a positive or historical truth of a given religion. In addition to the subjective element that will always be present in the artist's creation, sacred art also has an objective quality that transcends the individual's forms of expression, and, for this reason, it can be appreciated by anyone who is familiar with its religious theme.[2]

Such a distinction between religious art and sacred art is not just a nuance. Sacred art specifically aims at a visible translation of a reality that transcends the limits of human individuality. On the part of the artist, this requires an openness to be formed by the faith of the Church. This has important consequences for its modes of expression, as Joseph Ratzinger observes in the chapter entitled "The Question of Images" of his book *The Spirit of the Liturgy*:

> No sacred art can come from an isolated subjectivity. . . . The freedom of art, which is also necessary in the more narrowly circumscribed realm of sacred art, is not a matter of do-as-you-please. . . . Without faith there is no art commensurate with the liturgy (*Ohne Glauben gibt es keine der Liturgie gemäße Kunst*).[3]

On a similar note, the theologian and art critic Carlo Chenis notes with reference to *Sacrosanctum Concilium*, no. 122, that sacred art is the "summit" of religious art (the Latin text reads *culmen* here), because it is explicitly directed to the praise and glory of God. Chenis remarks that "religious art" becomes "sacred art" by virtue of being destined for the *sacrum*, which in the Christian context is not to be understood in a vague or generic sense, but as referring to the sacred liturgy. Hence sacred art is distinguished as being at

[2] E. Cattaneo, *Arte e liturgia dalle origini al Vaticano II* (Milan: Vita e pensiero, 1982), 8.

[3] J. Ratzinger, *The Spirit of the Liturgy*, trans. J. Saward (San Francisco: Ignatius Press, 2000), 134 (JRCW 11:83).

the service of the Church's divine worship.[4] The artist and art historian Rodolfo Papa has found a fine analogy when he says that between a work of religious art and a work of sacred art there is the same relationship that unites and distinguishes a poem that speaks of God and a prayer.[5]

There is another important dimension that needs to be highlighted: sacred art is "popular" because it has the capacity to be understood by all the faithful and to touch their hearts. In the history of the Church, sacred art provided a visualization of biblical narratives and of the lives of the saints at a time when most people were illiterate and access to books was restricted to those with considerable material resources. This extraordinary achievement is not adequately conveyed by the expression "Poor Man's Bible"; rather, sacred images enable the faithful to experience the history of salvation and the communion of saints as present in the Church's worship. For this reason it remains valid for today that sacred art can never be the domain of a self-declared elite or avant-garde.

Sacred Art in the Church's Teaching

The *Compendium* to the *Catechism of the Catholic Church*, published in 2005, uses masterpieces of sacred art from various cultural traditions to give a visual expression to the teachings

[4] C. Chenis, *Fondamenti teorici dell'arte sacra: Magistero post-conciliare* (Rome: Libreria Ateneo Salesiano, 1991), 25. Cattaneo, *Arte e liturgia*, 8, introduces a third category, "liturgical art", which follows the "fundamental rule of Christian worship, that is, *legem credendi lex statuat supplicandi*" (let the law of supplication manifest the law of belief) and can even be considered a constitutive part of the liturgy. However, Cattaneo's distinction between sacred art and liturgical art does not seem compelling, since it is common to both of them that they express the *lex credendi*.

[5] R. Papa, "Riflessioni sui fondamenti dell'arte sacra", *Euntes docete* 3 (1999): 327–41, at 331.

of the Catholic faith. Joseph Ratzinger, as cardinal, wrote in his introduction to the *Compendium*, which he approved as pope:

> The centuries-old conciliar tradition teaches us that images are also a preaching of the Gospel. Artists in every age have offered the principal facts of the mystery of salvation to the contemplation and wonder of believers by presenting them in the splendour of colour and in the perfection of beauty. It is an indication of how today more than ever, in a culture of images, a sacred image can express much more than what can be said in words, and be an extremely effective and dynamic way of communicating the Gospel message.[6]

As is indicated here, the Fathers of the Church, ecumenical councils, especially the Second Council of Nicaea in 787, provincial and diocesan synods, and individual bishops have dedicated considerable attention to questions of sacred art, especially the use of images. Moreover, as clients of churches or of works of sacred art, popes and bishops have also given specific instructions to artists. To single out one example, the sixteenth century was a period not only of stupendous artistic creativity but also of intense reflection on the fine arts. Among those who shaped this debate were several prominent ecclesiastics connected with Saint Philip Neri (1515–1595) and the Congregation of the Oratory: the cardinals and reforming bishops Saint Charles Borromeo (1538–1584), Federico Borromeo (1564–1631), Agostino Valier (1531–1606), and Gabriele Paleotti (1522–1597).[7] In his *Discourse on Images Sacred and Profane* of 1582, Paleotti

[6] J. Ratzinger, Introduction to *Compendium: Catechism of the Catholic Church* (Washington, D.C.: United States Conference of Catholic Bishops, 2006) xvii.

[7] See C. Hecht, *Katholische Bildertheologie im Zeitalter von Gegenreformation und Barock: Studien zu Traktaten von Johannes Molanus, Gabriele Paleotti und anderen Autoren*, 2nd ed., rev. and enlarged (Berlin: Gebr. Mann, 2012).

provides a description of sacred art in accordance with the norms established by the Council of Trent, in which he participated. The erudite prelate argued that the art of painting originally had the sole purpose of representing visible reality; in the context of the sacred, however, it acquires a higher end, which is aiming at eternal glory by turning souls away from vice and leading them to the worship of God.[8]

The right use of images remained a concern of the Church's pastors in the centuries after Trent, and one of the most significant documents was Pope Benedict XIV's Brief *Sollicitudini Nostrae* of 1745, which provided a concise summary of the preceding debates. This papal document was issued to settle the controversies caused by the visions of the Bavarian nun Crescenzia of Kaufbeuren (1682–1744, canonized in 2001) of the Holy Spirit as a handsome young man. These visions became very popular, especially through the printing of devotional images of this type. Benedict XIV used this occasion to offer general principles on the representation of God in sacred art and to give particular directives on how the Blessed Trinity should and should not be depicted. He condemned the images inspired by the Bavarian visionary as well as popular paintings of the Trinity showing a man with three heads or three faces. The learned pope insisted that representations of the Trinity should have some biblical reference and permitted the image of God the Father inspired by the figure of "the ancient of days" (Dan 7:9). Above all he insisted that the Father and the Son should be

[8] "La Pittura, dunque, in origine aveva il solo scopo di rendere verosimile la realtà, ora per mezzo delle Virtù, si veste di un nuovo valore e, oltre a rendere verosimile la realtà, si eleva ad un fine maggiore mirando alla gloria eterna, distogliendo gli uomini dal vizio e conducendoli al culto di Dio": G. Paleotti, *Discorso intorno alle immagini sacre e profane (1582)*, ed. S. Della Torre (Vatican City: Libreria Editrice Vaticana, 2002), libro I, cap. 19: "Fine particolare specifico delle immagini cristiane", 67.

depicted as two separate persons and that the Holy Spirit should be shown in the form of a dove.[9]

It was only in the twentieth century that the Supreme Magisterium of the Catholic Church made general pronouncements about sacred art and its relationship with the sacred liturgy. The first papal document in question was Pius XII's encyclical *Mediator Dei* of 1947, to be followed by the Second Vatican Council's Constitution *Sacrosanctum Concilium*. It is of course not surprising that these documents, being concerned with the liturgy in its various aspects, also touch upon art that is destined for the Church's solemn worship. However, it would seem that the very fact of such a general treatment of sacred art is also indicative of a crisis —a crisis that was seen clearly by Pope Paul VI, who in his *Homily to Artists* given in the Sistine Chapel on May 7, 1964, lamented the rift between the Church and the arts, which had adopted the "language of Babylon" and were no longer able to express the sacred.[10]

[9] Benedict XIV, Brief *Sollicitudini Nostrae* (1745); see F. Boespflug, *Dieu dans l'art: "Sollicitudini Nostrae" de Benoît XIV (1745) e l'affaire Crescence de Kaufbeuren* (Paris: Cerf, 1984).

[10] Paul VI, *Homily at the "Mass of the Artists" in the Sistine Chapel* (May 7, 1964): "Ci permettete una parola franca? Voi ci avete un po' abbandonato, siete andati lontani, a bere ad altre fontane, alla ricerca sia pure legittima di esprimere altre cose; ma non più le nostre. . . . Voi sapete che portiamo una certa ferita nel cuore, quando vi vediamo intenti a certe espressioni artistiche che offendono noi, tutori dell'umanità intera, della definizione completa dell'uomo, della sua sanità, della sua stabilità. . . . Qualche volta dimenticate il canone fondamentale della vostra consacrazione all'espressione; non si sa cosa dite, non lo sapete tante volte anche voi: ne segue un linguaggio di Babele . . . e allora restiamo sorpresi ed intimiditi e distaccati". See also Paul VI's *Message to Artists at the closing of the Second Vatican Council* (December 8, 1965). Cf. R. van Bühren, *Kunst und Kirche im 20. Jahrhundert: Die Rezeption des Zweiten Vatikanischen Konzils* (Paderborn: Schöningh, 2008).

Crisis of Art—Crisis of Beauty

The crisis identified by Paul VI goes far beyond the question of art in the ecclesial realm. In a recent essay with the suggestive title "The End of Art", Roger Kimball comments wryly: "We behave as if art were something special, something important, something spiritually refreshing; but, when we canvas the roster of distinguished artists today, what we generally find is far from spiritual, and certainly far from refreshing." The cultural avant-garde, Kimball continues, "has transformed the practice of art into a purely negative enterprise, in which art is either oppositional or it is nothing. Celebrity replaces aesthetic achievement as the goal of art."[11] In fact, we are living through a cultural crisis that rejects the very concept of "fine arts", which is invoked in *Sacrosanctum Concilium* as the foundation of sacred art. At the heart of this rejection, there is the loss or rather the denial of beauty itself. To quote Kimball again, "large precincts of the art world have jettisoned the link between art and beauty."[12] This acute analysis of the predicament of art in the contemporary world is shared, at least in part, by art critics of renown, such as Stefano Zecchi[13] and Jean Clair, who made an outstanding contribution to the "Courtyard of the Gentiles" in Paris on March 25, 2011. This initiative of Benedict XVI evokes the Temple in Jerusalem, which had a courtyard for the gentiles who were at some distance

[11] R. Kimball, "The End of Art", *First Things* 184 (June/July 2008): 27–31, at 27; an extended version of this essay has been published as "The Vocation of Art", in *Religion and the American Future*, ed. C. DeMuth and Y. Levin (Washington, D.C.: AEI Press, 2008), 179–207.

[12] Kimball, "End of Art", 27.

[13] S. Zecchi, *L'artista armato: Contro i crimini della modernità* (Milan: Mondadori, 1998).

from the sanctuary but still related to it. They were not quite ready to cross the threshold, but they were not completely removed from it, either. This idea of a contemporary "Courtyard of the Gentiles" includes a re-launch of the dialogue between the Church and the arts. On this occasion, Clair gave a very remarkable analysis of the state of the arts in the contemporary world especially with regard to the sacred and did not spare his criticism for certain forms of artistic expression that have been admitted into churches, providing examples that are only the more drastic manifestations of a wider problem. Clair did not hide his perplexity about these phenomena, when he concluded: "God without Beauty is more incomprehensible than Beauty without God."[14]

By doing so, Clair evoked the Catholic and Orthodox tradition, where beauty is understood as an ontological and, ultimately, a theological category. Benedict XVI called artists "custodians of beauty",[15] as Paul VI had done before him. The search for beauty has nothing to do with mere aestheticism or flight from reason, because, from the divine perspective, beauty, along with truth and the good, is convertible with being and is there numbered among the "transcendentals".[16] Hence, art as the expression of the beautiful has the

[14] J. Clair, "Culte de l'Avant-Garde e culture de mort", available on http://chiesa.espresso.repubblica.it/articolo/1348110?fr=y; for extracts in English, see http://chiesa.espresso.repubblica.it/articolo/1348149?eng=y (accessed August 2, 2013); cf. also his *Considérations sur l'état des beaux-arts: Critique de la modernité* (Paris: Gallimard, 1983).

[15] Benedict XVI, *Address at the Meeting with Artists in the Sistine Chapel* (November 21, 2009).

[16] Cf. F. A. Murphy, *Christ the Form of Beauty: A Study in Theology and Literature* (London: Continuum, 1995), 213: "St Bonaventure is the first among the Franciscans to *list* beauty as a transcendental property of being. He lists four transcendentals: being, truth, goodness and beauty. Beauty never appears in the lists of transcendentals composed by the Dominican scholastics, Albert the Great and St Thomas Aquinas. However . . . they both succumb

capacity of showing reality to us, and sacred art in particular reveals divine beauty.[17] There is a remarkable passage in the *Compendium* of the *Catechism of the Catholic Church* that sums up this theological concept of beauty. What is especially noteworthy is that this article is found in the section of the catechism about the eighth commandment: "You shall not bear false witness against your neighbor". In response to question no. 526, "What relationship exists between truth, beauty and sacred art?", the *Compendium* says concisely:

> The truth is beautiful, carrying in itself the splendour of spiritual beauty. In addition to the expression of the truth in words there are other complementary expressions of the truth, most specifically in the beauty of artistic works. These are the fruit both of talents given by God and of human effort. *Sacred art* by being true and beautiful should evoke and glorify the mystery of God made visible in Christ, and lead to the adoration and love of God, the Creator and Saviour, who is the surpassing, invisible Beauty of Truth and Love.[18]

In the modern context, it is precisely the transcendent dimension of beauty as being convertible with truth and goodness that is contested. Beauty has been divested of its ontological significance; it has been "emancipated" from the

---

to its lure in their respective Commentaries on *The Divine Names* of Pseudo-Dionysius. In these texts, each of these writes speaks of the universal extent of beauty, and names God as its first cause." Francesca Murphy's book is an insightful treatment of the subject, with ample reference to the relevant twentieth-century debates, to which also Jacques Maritain and Étienne Gilson contributed.

[17] For an Islamic perspective on the beauty of God, cf. N. Kermani, *Gott ist schön: Das ästhetische Erleben des Koran* (Munich: C. H. Beck, 1999).

[18] *Compendium: Catechism of the Catholic Church*, no. 526, referring to nos. 2500–2503 of the *Catechism of the Catholic Church*, 2nd ed. (Vatican City and Washington, D.C.: Libreria Editrice Vaticana, 2000).

order of being and has been reduced to an aesthetic experience or, indeed, to a matter of "feeling". The disastrous consequences of this revolution are not limited to the art world. Rather, along with the loss of beauty, we have also lost goodness and truth, as the Swiss theologian Hans Urs von Balthasar describes lucidly:

> In a world without beauty—even if people cannot dispense with the word and constantly have it on the tip of their tongues in order to abuse it—in a world which is perhaps not wholly without beauty, but which can no longer see it or reckon with it: in such a world the good also loses its attractiveness, the self-evidence of why it must be carried out. Man stands before the good and asks himself why *it* must be done and not rather its alternative, evil. For this, too, is a possibility, and even the more exciting one: Why not investigate Satan's depths?[19]

One result of this separation of beauty from truth and the good has been the phenomenon described by the Italian philosopher Remo Bodei as the "apotheosis of the ugly".[20] By this he means an aesthetic theory and practice that rejects anything beautiful as a deception and holds that only the representation of what is crude, vulgar, and low is true. This school of thought has had an effect on liturgy as well as on sacred art and architecture. In the last forty years it has not been a rare thing to hear that beauty is not an appropriate category of divine worship, and a considerable part of the Church's cultural and artistic patrimony has been squandered in the name of honesty and simplicity. Generally speaking, iconoclasm seems to be a constant temptation for

[19] H. U. von Balthasar, *The Glory of the Lord*, vol. 1, *Seeing the Form*, trans. E. Leiva-Merikakis (San Francisco: Ignatius Press, 1982), 19.

[20] R. Bodei, *Le forme del bello* (Bologna: Il Mulino, 1995), 120.

theologians, and it recurs again and again in the history of the Church, not least in the twentieth century.

Of course, the Catholic tradition also knows of a false kind of beauty that does not lift men up toward God and his eternal kingdom but, instead, drags them down and stirs disordered desires for power, possession, and pleasure. The Book of Genesis makes clear that it was such false beauty that in some sense caused original sin. After the serpent provoked Eve into having rebellious thoughts against God, she saw that the fruit of the tree in the midst of the garden was fair to the eyes and a delight to behold (Gen 3:6). As Kimball notes, "If beauty can use art to express truth, art can also use beauty to create charming fabrications. . . . Instead of directing our attention beyond sensible beauty toward its supersensible source, art can fascinate us with beauty's apparently self-sufficient presence; it can counterfeit being in lieu of revealing it." Kimball also observes that "Western thinking about art has tended to oscillate between adulation and deep suspicion", and he refers to the Russian writer Fyodor Dostoevsky (1821–1881), who in his novel *The Brothers Karamazov* (1880) has Mitya Karamazov say: "Beauty is the battlefield where God and the devil war for the soul of man."[21]

Ever since the turn to the subjective that results from the Enlightenment philosophy of Immanuel Kant and the Romantic movement, it has been extremely difficult, if not impossible, to restate the metaphysical foundations of beauty. I consider a fine book by Roger Scruton an excellent example of this aporia. Scruton is aware of the need to recover the metaphysical foundations of beauty, which were eroded in

[21] Kimball, "End of Art", 28; the quotation is from F. Dostoevsky, *The Brothers Karamazov*, bk. 3, chap. 3.

the eighteenth century, when "aesthetics" became a separate philosophical discipline, but in the end, he cannot do so and must limit himself to the judgment of taste.[22] Certainly, an education of taste would go a long way, but, in the end, *de gustibus non est disputandum*. In other words, a well-honed aesthetic instinct cannot provide foundations stable enough or strong enough to rebuild the metaphysical underpinnings of the arts today.

Elements of a theological response to this question are found in a renewed appreciation of the Christian tradition. In a well-known passage from his novel *The Idiot* (1869), the same Dostoevsky has his Christ-like hero, Prince Myshkin, say, "I believe the world will be saved by beauty." Not any beauty is meant here, but the redemptive beauty of Christ. In a profound reflection on this subject, written in 2002 for the annual *Communion and Liberation* meeting in Rimini, the then-Cardinal Ratzinger comments on Psalm 45(44), which praises the king at the occasion of his wedding and exalts his bride. In the exegetical tradition of the Church, this lyrical psalm has been read as a representation of Christ's spousal relationship with the Church and the description of the bridegroom as "the fairest of the sons of men" as Christ himself. Where the psalm declares that "grace is poured upon [his] lips", this is taken to refer to the beauty of his words, the glory of his proclamation. Ratzinger notes that it is "not merely the external beauty of the Redeemer's appearance that is praised: rather, the beauty of truth appears in him, the beauty of God himself, who powerfully draws us and inflicts on us the wound of Love".[23] This beauty attracts us

[22] R. Scruton, *Beauty* (Oxford: Oxford University Press, 2009).

[23] J. Ratzinger, "Wounded by the Arrow of Beauty: The Cross and the New 'Aesthetics' of Faith", in Ratzinger, *On the Way to Jesus Christ*, trans. M.J. Miller (San Francisco: Ignatius Press, 2005), 32–41, at 32–33.

and makes us join the procession of Christ's Mystical Bride, which is the Church, going out to meet the Bridegroom.

Presenting us with a stark contrast, the Church applies to the same Christ, who is praised as the "fairest of men", the words of Isaiah 53:2: "He had no form or comeliness that we should look at him, and no beauty that we should desire him." This is done in remembrance of his Passion and shows the "paradoxical beauty" of Christ, which implies a contrast but not a contradiction. As Ratzinger observes, we come to know that "the beauty of truth also involves wounds, pain, and even the obscure mystery of death and that this can only be found in accepting pain, not in ignoring it."[24] The totality of Christ's beauty is revealed to us when we contemplate the disfigured image of the crucified Savior, which shows us his "love to the end" (cf. Jn 13:1). This is the beauty that will save the world, the redemptive beauty of Christ, crucified and glorified. It shines forth with particular splendor in the saints but is also reflected in the works of art the faith has generated. The masterpieces of sacred art have the power to lift our hearts to higher things and lead us beyond ourselves to an encounter with God, who is Beauty itself.

As pope, Joseph Ratzinger more than once expressed his profound conviction that the predicaments of today's world call for a "widening of the horizon of reason". Ever since the Enlightenment, and to some extent already before, reason has been narrowed to mere scientific and technical rationality: its sphere is only that which can be counted or measured. Benedict XVI is confident that religion can make an essential contribution to opening up this limited conception of reason, and the arts have an important part to play

[24] Ibid., 34.

in this. He even sees in the beauty that the faith has brought forth the true apology of Christianity. Rational argument remains important and indispensable, but the encounter with the beauty of God, especially through the arts, can today speak with much greater immediacy and effectiveness.[25]

Both as a theologian and as pope, he recommended Hans Urs von Balthasar's great project of theological aesthetics.[26] His own comments would seem to complement the observations of the Swiss theologian cited above. It should be added here that for Benedict XVI, this beauty does not remain an abstract concept but is manifest especially in the sacred liturgy, as he affirmed during his visit to the Cistercian Abbey of Heiligenkreuz in Austria in September 2007:

> The interior disposition of each priest, and of each consecrated person, must be that of "putting nothing before the divine Office". The beauty of this inner attitude will find expression in the beauty of the liturgy, so that wherever we join in singing, praising, exalting and worshipping God, a little bit of heaven will become present on earth. . . . I ask you to celebrate the sacred liturgy with your gaze fixed on God within the communion of saints, the living Church of every time and place, so that it will truly be an expression

[25] Cf. Benedict XVI, *Meeting with the Clergy of the Diocese of Bolzano-Bressanone* (August 6, 2008) and *Message on the Occasion of the 13th Public Conference of the Pontifical Academies* (November 24, 2008).

[26] See Ratzinger, "Wounded by the Arrow of Beauty", 36–37, and Benedict XVI, *Message for the Centenary of the Birth of Fr Hans Urs von Balthasar* (October 6, 2005), where he comments that Balthasar "made the mystery of the Incarnation the privileged subject of his study, seeing the *Easter triduum*—as he significantly entitled one of his writings—as the most expressive form of God's entrance into human history. In Jesus' death and Resurrection, in fact, the mystery of God's Trinitarian love is revealed in all its fullness. The reality of faith finds here its matchless *beauty*." Cf. the richly documented study of the subject by R. Viladesau, *Theological Aesthetics: God in Imagination, Beauty, and Art* (Oxford and New York: Oxford University Press, 1999).

of the sublime beauty of the God who has called men and women to be his friends![27]

Criteria for a Renewal of Sacred Art—Rereading Sacrosanctum Concilium

Given the predicament of sacred art in the context of modernity, it would seem urgent to find criteria for its renewal. However, when any such criteria are proposed in the present intellectual climate, they are often met with the objection that they place undue limits on the free exercise of artistic creativity. At this point in theological debates, reference is usually made to the following passage from *Sacrosanctum Concilium*:

> The Church has not adopted any particular style of art as her very own; she has admitted styles from every period according to the natural talents and circumstances of peoples, and the needs of the various rites. Thus, in the course of the centuries, she has brought into being a treasury of art which must be very carefully preserved. The art of our own days, coming from every race and region, shall also be given free scope in the Church, provided that it adorns the sacred buildings and holy rites with due reverence and honor; thereby it is enabled to contribute its own voice to that wonderful chorus of praise in honor of the Catholic faith sung by great men in times gone by.[28]

The opening phrase stating that the Church "has not adopted any particular style of art as her very own (*Ecclesia nullum artis stilum veluti proprium habuit*)" holds the hermeneutical key to the whole paragraph and requires a very careful

[27] Benedict XVI, *Address at Heiligenkreuz Abbey* (September 9, 2007).
[28] *Sacrosanctum Concilium*, no. 123.

reading.[29] Obviously, there is a plurality of styles in the Western tradition of sacred art and architecture, and no one particular style can be promoted as canonical. Saint Charles Borromeo's concern for the order and decorum of liturgical celebrations is manifest in his detailed instructions about church building and furnishing. These instructions served as a model for the Catholic Reform after Trent, but they did not determine any artistic style.[30] The Byzantine tradition, by contrast, has very clearly defined rules for artistic and architectural expression in the realms of the sacred, creating a precise "language" of symbolic meaning to be read and understood by the faithful. The development of this artistic language, which took place over many centuries, culminated in the codification of its "grammar", or governing rules, at the Council of Moscow in 1551, also known as the "Council of the Hundred Canons". Even more so, Islamic architecture has developed a rigid canon that allows for relatively little adaption to local cultures and makes a mosque immediately recognizable wherever it stands throughout the world.

[29] An example of misreading this statement is found in *Sing to the Lord: Music in Divine Worship* (Washington, D.C.: USCCB Publishing, 2008), a good document in many ways. However, no. 136 quotes the passage in question and concludes that, for this reason, "in recent times, the Church has consistently recognized and freely welcomed the use of various styles of music as an aid to liturgical worship." Above all, the quotation from *Sacrosanctum Concilium* is taken out of context: it is from the seventh chapter on "Sacred Art and Sacred Furnishings", while the sixth chapter of the Constitution is specifically dedicated to sacred music and presents clear criteria, with Gregorian chant being exalted as "proper" to the Roman liturgy (see especially no. 116, but also no. 112). This has recently been restated by Benedict XVI in his Post-Synodal Apostolic Exhortation *Sacramentum Caritatis* on the Eucharist as the Source and Summit of the Church's Life and Mission (February 22, 2007), no. 42. See the pertinent observations of W. P. Mahrt, "Commentary on *Sing to the Lord*", in Mahrt, *The Musical Shape of the Liturgy* (2008; Richmond, Va.: Church Music Association of America, 2012), 165–78, at 176.

[30] See Hecht, *Katholische Bildertheologie*, 20.

Thus it would be erroneous to postulate a single canonical style in the Western tradition, as has been done, for instance, by the great English Catholic architect Augustus Welby Pugin (1812–1852). Pugin extolled the liturgy, art, and architecture of the Gothic period as normative, whereas he considered classical forms in church building "a monstrous absurdity, which has originated in the blind admiration of modern times for every thing Pagan, to the prejudice and overthrow of Christian art and propriety".[31] As Sheridan Gilley comments, from the high medieval perspective Pugin had adopted, "anything later, from Saint Peter's in Rome to the smallest Baroque candlestick, was the product of the corruption of the church by Renaissance paganism."[32] To many of his contemporaries, Pugin's principles seemed compelling, because they implied that there "is the most intimate connection between a religion and culture and its outward expression, and [that] the Gothic was the only architectural and artistic style which Christendom had created for itself".[33]

Pugin was part of a wider cultural movement in Catholicism that sought to renew its artistic and architectural expression after the collapse of the Church in many parts of Europe in the wake of the French Revolution and the Napoleonic Wars. The turn toward the Middle Ages received a strong impetus from the Romantic movement, as did the rebirth of Catholicism in general. In many European countries,

[31] A. W. N. Pugin, *The True Principles of Pointed or Christian Architecture* (London: John Neale, 1841; reprinted with an introduction by R. O'Donnell, Leominster: Gracewing, 2003), 3.

[32] S. Gilley, "Newman, Pugin and the Architecture of the English Oratory", in *Modern Christianity and Cultural Aspirations*, ed. D. Bebbington and T. Larsen (London and New York: Sheffield Academic Press, 2003), 98–123, at 102.

[33] Ibid., 103.

Gothic was promoted as *the* Catholic style, and, as a consequence, the Baroque decorations of medieval cathedrals such as Bamberg were removed.[34] The statues of the apostles in the Siena cathedral by Giuseppe Mazzuoli (1644–1725), a disciple of Bernini, fell victim to the medieval fashion and were sold to the London Oratorians, who placed them into their neo-Renaissance church in the Brompton Road.[35] There are many examples of this "purification" of medieval churches, leading far into the twentieth century, when, for instance, many Puglian-Romanesque churches of Southern Italy were stripped of their Baroque interiors. However, what distinguishes Pugin is the rigor with which he proposed the Gothic as the canonical style of Catholic architecture. Sheridan Gilley's insightful comments are worth quoting in full:

> Indeed Pugin was a revolutionary modern in his underlying principles, being among the first to proclaim what have become some of the central arguments of the modern movement in architecture, that every part of the building should be functional, and be morally honest and in accordance with "*convenience, construction, or propriety*", so that decoration, if any, should be honestly subordinate to structure and illustrate it.[36]

[34] Cf. R. Baumgärtel-Fleischmann, *Die Altäre des Bamberger Domes von 1012 bis zur Gegenwart*, in collaboration with B. Neundorfer, B. Schemmel, W. Milutzki, Veröffentlichungen des Diözesan-Museums Bamberg 4 (Bamberg: Bayerische Verlagsanstalt, 1987).

[35] A. Laing, "Baroque Sculpture in a Neo-Baroque Setting", in *The London Oratory: Centenary 1884–1984*, ed. M. Napier and A. Laing (London: Trefoil, 1984), 56–83.

[36] Gilley, "Newman, Pugin and the Architecture of the English Oratory", 110.

These principles were an adaptation of the classical Vitruvian formula of strength, utility, and beauty;[37] however, as Gilley observes, Pugin's understanding of them

> led straight on to the Bauhaus and Le Corbusier, who took one step further in rejecting decoration altogether. In the same way, Pugin in his demand for the destruction of anything classical or Baroque, as departing from his "true principles", was very like the modern architect or liturgist who in the name of one principle demands that everything old be swept away.[38]

It goes without saying that the magnificent churches Pugin actually designed bear hardly any resemblance to the edifices of the modernist style of architecture that flourished in the twentieth century. What is noted here by Gilley and others is a striking similarity of architectural principles: the categories of functionality and decoration are invested with *moral* significance.

Pugin found himself in conflict with the newly founded Congregation of the Oratory of Saint Philip Neri in England over architectural matters. It is worth pondering John Henry Newman's perceptive critique that there had been no "*uninterrupted tradition* of Gothic architecture from the time it was introduced till the present day. . . . Mr Pugin is notoriously engaged in a revival." As Gilley, Newman's authoritative biographer, comments, "Pugin's conception of revival contradicted Newman's own idea of doctrinal development,

[37] Marcus Vitruvius Pollio, *De architectura*, I, III, 2: "Haec autem ita fieri debent, ut habeatur ratio firmitatis, utilitatis, venustatis."

[38] Gilley, "Newman, Pugin and the Architecture of the English Oratory", 110; see also D. Watkin, *Morality and Architecture: The Development of a Theme in Architectural History and Theory from the Gothic Revival to the Modern Movement* (Oxford: Clarendon Press, 1977).

in which there had to be both a continuity and permanence in what was essential, while the Church, wrote Newman, was 'ever modifying, adapting, varying her discipline and ritual, according to the times.'"[39] Newman advocated an eclectic freedom that embraced various historical styles of sacred art and architecture. The irony of history is that, just as Pugin wanted only Gothic as the one canonical style of church building, today it seems that—not *de iure* but *de facto*, in most of the Catholic world—the "International Style" of modernism has become the "officially sanctioned style of the Church", a style that allows as little freedom to other forms of expression as Pugin did with his Gothic.[40]

Resuming our reading of *Sacrosanctum Concilium*, there can be no doubt that sacred art and architecture in the West owes its richness to the variety of its styles; to take up a line from the Constitution on the Sacred Liturgy, art has been given "free scope in the Church" (*SC* 123), and the result was a stunning surge of creativity. However, it would seem that this creativity always existed within certain coordinates, and I should like to argue that this is what the same document

[39] Ibid., 109; quotes from J. H. Newman's letter to A. Phillipps De Lisle of June 15, 1848: *The Letters and Diaries of John Henry Newman*, vol. 12: *Rome to Birmingham January 1847 to December 1848*, ed. C. S. Dessain (London: Nelson, 1962), 220–22. In the same letter, Newman wrote: "I begged him (Pugin) to see the Oratory of the Chiesa Nuova, he gave me no hope he would do so. Now is it wonderful that I prefer St Philip to Mr Pugin?"

[40] D. Stroik, "The Roots of Modernist Church Architecture", *Adoremus Bulletin* 3 (1997) online edition: http://adoremus.org/1097-Stroik.html (accessed July 6, 2015). Stroik observes: "To many educated observers, it would seem that the reductionist buildings commissioned for Roman Catholic worship today are the direct corollary of Church teaching, modern liturgical studies and contemporary theology." For further criticism of contemporary church architecture, see also S. J. Schloeder, *Architecture in Communion: Implementing the Second Vatican Council through Liturgy and Architecture* (San Francisco: Ignatius Press, 1998); M. Doorly, *No Place for God: The Denial of the Transcendent in Modern Church Architecture* (San Francisco: Ignatius Press, 2007).

meant when it welcomed contemporary art "that adorns the sacred buildings and holy rites with due reverence and honor" (*SC* 123). This will become clearer when *Sacrosanctum Concilium* is read together with Pope Pius XII's encyclical *Mediator Dei*, applying a "hermeneutic of continuity" as presented by Benedict XVI in his speech to the Roman Curia of December 22, 2005.[41] *Mediator Dei* teaches on sacred art:

> Recent works of art which lend themselves to the materials of modern composition, should not be universally despised and rejected through prejudice. Modern art should be given free scope in the due and reverent service of the Church and the sacred rites, provided that they preserve a correct balance between styles tending neither to extreme realism nor to excessive "symbolism", and that the needs of the Christian community are taken into consideration rather than the particular taste or talent of the individual artist. Thus modern art will be able to join its voice to that wonderful choir of praise to which have contributed, in honor of the Catholic faith, the greatest artists throughout the centuries.[42]

While Pius XII discusses the legitimate variety of styles in sacred art in terms that are very similar to those of *Sacrosanctum Concilium*, he sets two clear parameters, speaking of a "correct balance" that avoids certain extremes. Given the historical context, the reference to a mere imitation of nature[43]

[41] Benedict XVI introduced "the 'hermeneutic of reform', of renewal in the continuity of the one subject-Church which the Lord has given to us", in his *Christmas Address to the Members of the Roman Curia* (December 22, 2005). With reference to the liturgy in particular, he speaks of a "hermeneutic of continuity" in *Sacramentum Caritatis*, no. 3.

[42] Pius XII, Encyclical on the Sacred Liturgy *Mediator Dei* (November 20, 1947), no. 195.

[43] The Latin text of *Mediator Dei* says "*ad nudam . . . rerum imitationem*",

may be illustrated with reference to the monumental "Crucifixion of Christ" (1890) by the German artist Max Klinger. Because of its attention to historical detail, this painting achieves a deliberate rupture with the iconographic tradition of the subject. The fact that Christ was painted naked on the cross caused scandal when the work was first exhibited in Dresden in 1893. When, on the other hand, *Mediator Dei* speaks of "excessive symbolism", it would seem possible to connect this with certain examples of liturgical art produced by Benedictines in the nineteenth century. Thus the Beuron School tended toward a stylized and hieratic symbolism that is consciously modeled on ancient Egyptian and Greek art and pays great attention to geometric proportions. A good example of this style would be Peter (later Father Desiderius) Lenz' chapel of Saint Maurus on the grounds of Beuron Abbey, dating from 1868/1869.

While encouraging the search for a contemporary sacred art, Pius XII expresses the hope that "modern art will be able to join its voice to that wonderful choir of praise to which have contributed, in honor of the Catholic faith, the greatest artists throughout the centuries." The use of the metaphor "choir of praise" is significant here because it implies an existing structure and harmony into which new forms of sacred art will need to be integrated. From this perspective, it would seem obvious that certain artistic productions cannot be admitted into this "choir of praise". Thus *Mediator Dei* continues on a stronger note:

> Nevertheless, in keeping with the duty of Our office, We cannot help deploring and condemning those works of art, recently introduced by some, which seem to be a distor-

---

which is rendered rather loosely as "excessive realism" in the common English version of the encyclical.

> tion and perversion of true art and which at times openly shock Christian taste, modesty and devotion, and shamefully offend the true religious sense. These must be entirely excluded and banished from our churches, like "anything else that is not in keeping with the sanctity of the place" [*Code of Canon Law* 1917, can. 1178].[44]

Compare this with the very similar passage in the seventh chapter of *Sacrosanctum Concilium* on "Sacred Art and Sacred Furnishings":

> Let bishops carefully remove from the house of God and from other sacred places those works of artists which are repugnant to faith, morals, and Christian piety, and which offend true religious sense either by depraved forms or by lack of artistic worth, mediocrity and pretense.[45]

Thus the legitimate freedom of artistic expression in sacred art does not dispense us from searching for adequate criteria and then making an informed judgment about what kind of art is truly "in the due and reverent service of the church and the sacred rites" (*Mediator Dei*, no. 195) and "adorns the sacred buildings and holy rites with due reverence and honor" (*Sacrosanctum Concilium*, no. 123).[46] We should also bear in mind that the *Code of Canon Law* of 1917

[44] Pius XII, *Mediator Dei*, no. 195.

[45] *Sacrosanctum Concilium*, no. 124.

[46] See also the Second Vatican Council's Pastoral Constitution on the Church in the Modern World *Gaudium et Spes* (December 7, 1965), no. 62: "The Church acknowledges also new forms of art which are adapted to our age and are in keeping with the characteristics of various nations and regions. They may be brought into the sanctuary *when* they raise the mind to God, once the manner of expression is adapted and they are conformed to liturgical requirements" (emphasis added). The common English translation mistakenly reads "since" for the Latin "*cum*", which twists the meaning of the phrase. In accordance with other language versions of the text, this has been changed to "when".

contained clear prescriptions about sacred art and architecture, which provides a context for reading both documents. Thus can. 1164, §1, stipulated that Ordinaries, that is, above all diocesan bishops, should take care that, when a new church had to be built or an existing one had to be renovated, "the forms received from Christian tradition and the laws of sacred art are preserved".[47] Hence it would seem safe to assume that both Pius XII and the Fathers of Vatican II presuppose that new artistic forms must have a firm point of reference in the Church's great tradition. In the realm of sacred art, such limits are legitimate, and they are necessary. Even more, they help artistic creativity to widen its horizons. Artists who used to have important commissions from bishops or popes, such as Michelangelo Buonarotti in Rome, entered into relationships with their patrons, which could at times become difficult. However, such tensions proved to be immensely creative and opened up depths of artistic expression that otherwise might not have been reached. In other words, the Church has always nurtured artists and has brought out greatness in them that might not have manifested itself otherwise.

Recovering the Sacred Image

In his pontificate, Benedict XVI has recognized that now is a propitious moment for a renewed engagement of the Church in the artistic world. As Remo Bodei observes, modern art has exhausted itself in its project of "transcend-

[47] *Codex Iuris Canonici* 1917, can. 1164, §1: "Curent Ordinarii, audito etiam, si opus fuerit, peritorum consilio, ut in ecclesiarum aedificatione vel refectione serventur formae a traditione christiana receptae et artis sacrae leges." English trans.: *The 1917 or Pio-Benedictine Code of Canon Law in English Translation* (San Francisco: Ignatius Press, 2001), 397.

ing boundaries", because in the secularized West there are hardly any artistic rules or traditions left to break, the result being that gestures of protest and provocation have become empty and ephemeral.[48] Consequently, the modernist movement in art and architecture, which began with a vigorous secession from received artistic canons, is now, as Kimball notes, a tired repetition of what Marcel Duchamp and the Dadaists did a century ago.[49] On the other hand, outside the commercial centers of the contemporary art world there are promising developments, such as a reappraisal of twentieth-century art and a return to figurative painting and sculpture.[50]

A renewal of sacred art needs not only artists who follow their calling regardless of the rules of the market but also enlightened and courageous patrons. Many ecclesiastical clients seem to have lost the confidence to build up and occasionally to correct artists when they enter the realm of

[48] Bodei, *Le forme del bello*, 120: "L'ideale delle *belle arti* non è tuttavia tramontato neppure in seguito all'apparente apoteosi del brutto. Si assiste anzi, in questi ultimi tempi, al veloce congedo dalla adorniana fase del cordoglio, a una crescente insofferenza nei confronti dell'*arte brutta* e dello sperimentalismo esacerbato delle avanguardie. Il gesto di violare regole e tradizioni lascia ormai indifferenti: la sua eco si spegne presto nel frastuono dei linguaggi, degli stili, delle mode. Esistono rimozioni che non siano state rimosse? Si conoscono forme di negatività, di licenza, di trasgressione a cui sia stata negata la facoltà di esprimersi? Ora che quasi tutti i generi di provocazione sembrano esperiti ed esauriti, si vede bene che gli scandali o si dimenticano subito oppure, per durare appena qualche mese, hanno bisogno di venire fomentati in modo artificiale."

[49] Kimball, "End of Art", 27: "These days, the art world places a great premium on novelty. But here's the irony: Almost everything championed as innovative in contemporary art is essentially a tired repetition of gestures inaugurated by the likes of Marcel Duchamp, creator of the first bottle-rack masterpiece and the first urinal fountain."

[50] Cf. the collection of essays by M. Mosebach, *Du sollst dir ein Bild machen: Über alte und neue Meister* (Springe: zu Klampen, 2005).

the sacred. The progressive alienation between Christianity and the arts beginning with the Enlightenment and the French Revolution and culminating in the modernist movement of the twentieth century has made churchmen afraid of appearing out of touch with the contemporary world. As has been seen in the first chapter of this book, ritual forms (such as those in the sacred liturgy) can never be entirely contemporary, and hence any renewal of the Church's architectural and artistic expressions must retain visible continuity with those that have been received. More recently, there has been a fruitful collaboration between architects of the new classical movement and artists of a younger generation who have been trained in figurative painting and sculpture at small private academies in Florence. The sculptor Cody Swanson, for instance, has contributed to the remarkable project of resacralizing Sioux Falls Cathedral led by Duncan Stroik.[51]

The crisis of sacred art we are experiencing is above all a crisis of the sacred image. This is crucial for Christianity, which is an incarnational religion: the Word has become flesh, and so the transcendent, invisible God has become visible in Jesus of Nazareth. Hence the image is indispensable for its religious expression. However, in Joseph Ratzinger's analysis, the unprecedented domination of the material realm that man has achieved in this present age has brought about a materialistic world view that is blind to the questions of life that transcend this world. This "blindness of the spirit" has serious consequences for our apprehension of reality: on the one hand, images are ubiquitous and seem to have a far stronger impact on our minds than words; on

[51] See M. McDonald, "Creative Restoration", *Traditional Building* 25 (2012): 28–31.

the other hand, these images remain on the surface of appearance, that is, they do not go beyond that which can be immediately perceived by the senses; thus the transcendent dimension, which is so important for the sacred image, is no longer understood.[52]

As said at the outset of this chapter, sacred art can be described as being at the service of the Church's solemn public worship. Marcel Proust (1871–1922) argued that the aesthetic impression of the French cathedrals was inseparable from the liturgical ceremonies that were carried out in them.[53] In a similar vein, Joseph Ratzinger has observed in *The Spirit of the Liturgy*: "The great cultural tradition of the faith is home to a presence of immense power. What in museums is only a monument from the past, an occasion for mere nostalgic admiration, is constantly made present in the liturgy in all its freshness."[54] Hence a renewal of sacred art in the contemporary world will depend on a renewal of the sacred liturgy. Benedict XVI has taken decisive steps toward such a renewal, and we have reason to hope that its fruits will also be seen in sacred art and architecture.

As a cardinal, he has written of "the struggle—necessary in every generation—for the right understanding and worthy celebration of the sacred liturgy";[55] the same holds for sacred art and architecture. And as he has reminded us, at the beginning of this struggle there must be the realization

[52] Cf. Ratzinger, *Spirit of the Liturgy*, 130–31 (JRCW 11:80–81).

[53] M. Proust, "La Mort des cathédrales", *Le Figaro*, August 16, 1904: 3. This article was written at the height of the Dreyfus affair and shortly before the separation of church and state, when the religious use of the French cathedrals was threatened by the withdrawal of state subsidies.

[54] Ratzinger, *Spirit of the Liturgy*, 155 (JRCW 11:93).

[55] J. Ratzinger, preface to U. M. Lang, *Turning Towards the Lord: Orientation in Liturgical Prayer*, 2nd ed. (San Francisco: Ignatius Press, 2009), 9–12, at 12 (JRCW 11:395).

that art—like liturgy—"cannot be 'produced', as one contracts out and produces technical equipment. It is always a gift. . . . Before all things it requires the gift of a new kind of seeing. And so it would be worth our while to regain a faith that sees."[56]

[56] Ratzinger, *Spirit of the Liturgy*, 135 (JRCW 11:83).

V

Sacred Music: Between Theological Millstones

In his writings and speeches as pope, Benedict XVI often used musical imagery. In one of the first homilies of his pontificate, he called the Church a "symphony of witnesses" to the risen Christ, which is given a well-defined structure in the bishops as successors of the apostles under the primacy of the Bishop of Rome, the Successor of Peter.[1] This preference for music has its roots in Joseph Ratzinger's life, because from an early age he learned to love this form of art, especially the works of Wolfgang Amadeus Mozart.[2] He has shared this love with his brother, Georg, a priest and professional church musician, who worked for thirty years as director of the noted boys' choir of Regensburg cathedral.

Moreover, as a theologian Ratzinger engaged with questions of sacred music, and there is one particularly insightful contribution that I should like to take as the starting point for this chapter: it is the lecture "Theological Problems of Church Music", which he delivered at the Department of Church Music at the State Conservatory of Music in Stuttgart in January 1977. The text has since then been published several times and also an English translation.[3]

[1] Benedict XVI, *Homily at the Mass of Possession of the Chair of the Bishop of Rome* (May 7, 2005).

[2] See J. Ratzinger, *Milestones: Memoirs (1927–1977)*, transl. Erasmo Leiva-Merikakis. (San Francisco: Ignatius Press, 2005), 25.

[3] First published in German in 1978, an English translation is available

Sacred Music in the Postconciliar Reform

In this lecture, Ratzinger identified a crisis of sacred music, which he considered a consequence of the general predicament the Church was facing in the turbulent period following the Second Vatican Council and a reflection of the state of the arts in the contemporary world, which has affected music as well. Later he would return to this theme in his book *The Spirit of the Liturgy*, where he discusses the impact of modernity especially on the visual arts and the consequences for sacred art.[4] In the contribution of 1977, Ratzinger was above all concerned with the properly theological reasons for the crisis of church music; he observed that *musica sacra* seems to have fallen "between two opposing theological millstones", which agree only in grinding it down to dust.[5] Unlike in biblical times (see, for example Job 41:25; Is 47:2; Mt 18:6 and parallels), millstones are remote from most people's experience today. To appreciate the force of the metaphor, it will be useful to recall the sheer massiveness and grinding power of a millstone in turning hard substances into fine powder.

On the one side, then, there is the millstone of "puritanic functionalism of a liturgy conceived in purely pragmatic terms"; according to this idea, "the liturgical event . . . should be made non-cultic and returned to its simple point of departure, a community meal." This tendency goes

in *Sacred Music* 135 (2008): 5–14. A revised version is now included under the title "The Artistic Transposition of the Faith: Theological Problems of Church Music", in JRCW 11:480–93.

[4] See J. Ratzinger, *The Spirit of the Liturgy*, trans. J. Saward (San Francisco: Ignatius Press, 2000), 130–31 (JRCW 11:80–81). This question has been discussed above in chapter 4.

[5] Ratzinger, "Artistic Transposition of the Faith", 481.

together with a superficial reading of the principle of "active participation" (*participatio actuosa*), introduced by Pope Saint Pius X and championed by the Council's Constitution on the Sacred Liturgy. As regards church music, "active participation" is all too often taken to mean "the uniform activity of all present in the liturgy", which leaves no place any more for compositions that have a higher artistic standard, are to be sung by a schola or a choir, and are often accompanied by classical musical instruments. What remains licit is only congregational singing, "which in turn is not to be judged in terms of its artistic value but solely on the basis of its functionality, that is, its 'community-building' and participatory function".[6]

In a slightly earlier publication on the theological foundations of church music,[7] Ratzinger commented on some unilateral interpretations of the Council's Constitution on the Sacred Liturgy in this regard, such as Karl Rahner and Herbert Vorgrimler's *Short Compendium of the Council* (*Kleines Konzilskompendium*). In their commentary on *Sacrosanctum Concilium*, Rahner and Vorgrimler claim that traditional church music, "because of its—in the good sense—esoteric character", does not agree with "the essence of the liturgy" and "the highest principle of the liturgical reform", that is, the active participation of the faithful.[8] In the immediate postconciliar years, this was not an uncommon position among liturgists and theologians. Rembert Weakland, shortly before becoming abbot primate of the Benedictine

[6] Ibid.

[7] J. Ratzinger, "On the Theological Basis of Church Music", in JRCW 11:421–42 (first published in German in 1974).

[8] "Von ihrem im guten Sinn esoterischen Wesen her mit dem Wesen der Liturgie und dem obersten Grundsatz der Liturgiereform kaum in Übereinstimmung zu bringen": K. Rahner and H. Vorgrimler, *Kleines Konzilskompendium*, 2nd ed. (Freiburg: Herder, 1967), 48.

Confederation, called on sacred music to "deny her exalted position of being a 'telephone to the beyond'" (an expression coined by Friedrich Nietzsche in his polemic against Richard Wagner's *Parsifal*, which he considered a capitulation to Christianity).[9]

Such interpretations do not do justice to the sixth chapter "De musica sacra", of *Sacrosanctum Concilium*, which begins with a fulsome praise of the "musical tradition of the universal Church" and exalts it as "a treasure of inestimable value, greater than that of any other art". Sacred music enjoys a preeminent position because it gives artistic expression to the words of the rite; for this reason, it is "a necessary or integral part of the solemn liturgy" and has "a ministerial function" in it.[10] The Constitution on the Sacred Liturgy goes on to say:

> The treasure of sacred music is to be preserved and fostered with great care. Choirs must be diligently promoted, especially in cathedral churches; but bishops and other pastors of souls must be at pains to ensure that, whenever the sacred action is to be celebrated with song, the whole body of the faithful may be able to contribute that active participation which is rightly theirs, as laid down in Art. 28 and 30.[11]

Here the principle of "active participation" finds its expression in the demand that the faithful "may be able to contribute" by making responses and acclamations, by joining in the singing of psalms, antiphons, and hymns, as is specified earlier in the Constitution. However, this cannot

[9] R. Weakland, "Music as Art in Liturgy", *Worship* 41 (1967): 5–15. More such statements are documented by J. Hitchcock, *The Recovery of the Sacred* (New York: Seabury Press, 1974), 8–9.

[10] Second Vatican Council, Constitution on the Sacred Liturgy *Sacrosanctum Concilium* (December 4, 1963), no. 112.

[11] Ibid., no. 114.

be construed to exclude the singing of parts of the liturgy, especially on solemn occasions, by a choir or schola while the assembly is listening attentively and devoutly, which is also a form of participation. "Active participation" is not simply identical with external activity[12] and, in Pope John Paul II's words, "does not preclude the active passivity of silence, stillness and listening: indeed, it demands it".[13]

This understanding of *Sacrosanctum Concilium* would seem to be confirmed by the following paragraphs, where Gregorian chant is acclaimed as the proper chant (*proprium*) of the Roman liturgy; it should therefore "be given pride of place in liturgical services", without excluding "other kinds of sacred music, especially polyphony".[14] Moreover, the role of the pipe organ in the Latin Church is praised in even lyrical terms.[15] Particular appreciation is given to the religious music that is rooted in the traditions of peoples around the world, especially in mission countries.[16] Finally, composers are encouraged to see it as their calling "to cultivate sacred music and increase its store of treasures". New compositions should "have the qualities proper to genuine sacred music"; they should not just include works to be sung by "large choirs", but should also include works that meet the needs

[12] Cf. Benedict XVI, *Video Message at the Closing Mass of the 50th International Eucharistic Congress* (June 17, 2012): "Not infrequently, the revision of liturgical forms has remained at an external level, and 'active participation' has been confused with external activity."

[13] John Paul II, *Address to the Bishops of the Episcopal Conference of the United States of America (Washington, Oregon, Idaho, Montana and Alaska)* (October 9, 1998). The address continues: "Worshippers are not passive, for instance, when listening to the readings or the homily, or following the prayers of the celebrant, and the chants and music of the liturgy. These are experiences of silence and stillness, but they are in their own way profoundly active."

[14] *Sacrosanctum Concilium*, no. 116.

[15] Ibid., no. 120.

[16] Ibid., no. 119.

of "small choirs"—taking into account the limited resources of an average parish—and allow for the active participation of the whole assembly.[17]

Joseph Ratzinger sees in Rahner and Vorgrimler's reading of *Sacrosanctum Concilium* a typical example of the difference between what the Council texts say and what has been made of them in the postconciliar period.[18] Sacred music is just one area where this tension is manifest. In his first Christmas address to the members of the Roman Curia as pope, Benedict XVI identified and rejected an interpretation of the Council documents that follows a "hermeneutic of discontinuity and rupture" with the past and instead proposed a "hermeneutic of reform" or, as he elsewhere said with specific reference to the liturgy, a "hermeneutic of continuity".[19] It is his profound conviction that the Second Vatican Council is to be read in the context of the Church's bimillennial history of growth and development. Any liturgical renewal has as its guiding principle the general norm of *Sacrosanctum Concilium* that "there must be no innovations unless the good of the Church genuinely and certainly requires them; and care must be taken that any new forms adopted should in some way grow organically from forms already existing."[20] Nonetheless, the position formulated in Rahner and Vorgrimler's influential *Compendium* has had a lasting effect on church music throughout the world.[21]

[17] Ibid., no. 121.

[18] See Ratzinger, "On the Theological Basis of Church Music", 422–23.

[19] Benedict XVI, *Christmas Address to the Members of the Roman Curia* (December 22, 2005); Post-Synodal Apostolic Exhortation *Sacramentum Caritatis* on the Eucharist as the Source and Summit of the Church's Life and Mission (February 22, 2007), no. 3, n. 6.

[20] *Sacrosanctum Concilium*, no. 23.

[21] Not least in Italy; see J. Ratzinger, "The Image of the World and of Human Beings in the Liturgy and Its Expression in Church Music", in JRCW

Returning to Ratzinger's still topical analysis of 1977, on the other side there is the millstone of a "functionalism of accommodation", which has led to the appearance of new forms of choirs and orchestras that perform a generically "religious" music inspired by contemporary jazz and pop. He observes dryly that these ensembles "were certainly no less elitist than the old church choirs"; in other words, they did not allow for "active participation", either, but they "were not subjected to the same criticism" as traditional choirs.[22] The effect is the same as that of the tendency to conceive the liturgy in purely pragmatic terms: the traditional repertory of sacred music, from Gregorian chant to contemporary polyphonic compositions, is judged unsuitable for divine worship and is relegated at best to cathedral churches or in the end to the concert hall, where it may acquire "a more or less museum-like state of preservation"[23] or, one could

11:443–60 (first published 1985), at 444–47. This has been confirmed by the noted conductor Riccardo Muti in his "Introduzione" to the volume by J. Ratzinger (Benedetto XVI), *Lodate Dio con arte: Sul canto e sulla musica*, a cura di C. Carniato (Venice: Marcianum Press, 2010), 7–11.

[22] Ratzinger, "Artistic Transposition of the Faith", 481.

[23] Ibid. See also his perceptive comments in "Catholicism after the Council", trans. P. Russell, *The Furrow* 18 (1967): 11: "But as well as going back to the ancient liturgy, we can have the very opposite thing too, and that brings us to the other root from which the liturgical revival has sprung. Many will remember a time, not very many years ago, when the Gregorian chant was extolled as the only legitimate form of Church music, and against this there was no appeal. The orchestra was driven out of the church with a flaming sword—it was bad enough having Carolingian elements in the ancient Roman liturgy, but these orchestral Masses dating only from the Baroque age. After all! Now we see how the recent upsurge of enthusiasm for jazz music has opened the doors of the church to orchestras of vastly different style to those older orchestras, and it makes us wonder somehow whether we can give serious credence any more to all those things which claim to be an expression of liturgical renewal. Mere archaism does not help matters along but neither does mere modernisation."

add, may even develop into a secular ritual in the manner conceived by Richard Wagner for his *Bühnenweihfestspiel* ("a festival play for the consecration of the stage") *Parsifal*, a sublime, spiritual work that nonetheless, from a Christian perspective, occasionally borders on the blasphemous.

By analogy with the visual arts (see chapter 4), a distinction needs to be made between "religious music" and "sacred music". A work like Emilio de Cavalieri's *Rappresentatione di Anima, et di Corpo* (The portrayal of the soul and the body, 1600), which emerged from the Roman Congregation of the Oratory founded by Saint Philip Neri and is variously categorized in musical scholarship as either an opera or an oratorio, has an edifying religious content and a sacred character in the wider sense. However, it is not a musical setting of a liturgical text and was never intended for a specifically ritual context. The second criterion is no less significant than the first, as is shown by the example of Giuseppe Verdi's *Messa da Requiem*, completed in 1874 after the death of the novelist Alessandro Manzoni and first performed in his remembrance. Though setting the texts of the Mass for the Dead to music, the operatic dimensions of the work break any liturgical context and make it more suitably categorized as "religious music".[24]

A further distinction between "sacred music" and "liturgical music" will not be necessary if the character and scope of the former is properly understood. Alcuin Reid has found

[24] Curiously, the *Messa da Requiem* first resounded in the Church of San Marco, Milan, in the setting of a "dry mass" (*Messa secca*), where most of the Mass formulary would be used, except the Offertory, the Canon of the Mass, and the Communion. Cf. D. Rosen, *Verdi: Requiem*, Cambridge Music Handbooks (Cambridge: Cambridge University Press, 1995), 11–12. The "dry mass" had spread in the later Middle Ages as a form of devotion for funerals or marriages held in the afternoon, when (because of fasting rules) no Mass could be celebrated; it was proscribed in the Tridentine Reform.

a felicitous description when he notes that "sacred music is liturgical music" and adds: "music that has become liturgical, that has come to live harmoniously in the Church's public worship and . . . itself thereby shares in the sacrality of the liturgical action".[25]

Liturgy and Music: A Brief Historical Overview

The stark analysis the theologian Joseph Ratzinger presented some years ago is, I believe, still pertinent today. Church music is not in good shape—not everywhere, not in every parish or community, but on balance and in every corner of the Catholic world. However, the search for a remedy is not straightforward. In the history of the Church, there were often struggles to determine what justly and fittingly could be accepted as *musica sacra*. It might be argued that there is some precedent in the early Church for the attitude of "puritanic functionalism" toward music in the liturgy. Although the singing of psalms and, as a later development, hymns and canticles had a natural place in early Christian worship, there was no continuity with the musical practice of the Jerusalem Temple, with its festive character and its elaborate use of instruments, as we see described in various psalms.[26] Music in the Christian liturgy would rather seem

[25] A. Reid, "Sacred Music and Actual Participation in the Liturgy", in *Benedict XVI and Beauty in Sacred Music: Proceedings of the Third Fota International Liturgical Conference, 2010*, ed. J. E. Rutherford, Fota Liturgy Series (Dublin and New York: Four Courts Press and Scepter Publishers, 2012), 93–126, at 95.

[26] See J. McKinnon, *Music in Early Christian Literature*, Cambridge Readings in the Literature of Music (Cambridge: Cambridge University Press, 1987, reprinted 1993), 1–11, with further bibliography, and, by the same author,

to have continued the practice of the synagogue—if, indeed, the prayer service of the contemporary synagogue included music, which is a disputed point. At the same time, the early Christians were anxious to separate the use of music in their liturgy from that in pagan worship. A consequence of this distancing from both Temple worship and pagan ceremonies is the omission of instruments, which is still maintained in Eastern Christian traditions and has been a strong current in the Latin West as well, leaving aside the special place of the organ, which it gradually acquired beginning with the Carolingian period.[27]

Joseph Ratzinger insists that the sober character of liturgical music in early Christian worship cannot be interpreted as a rejection of the "sacred" and "cultic" dimension of music in favor of a more communitarian and indeed quotidian approach. Rather, it would reflect the nuanced sense of sacrality that is found in the comments of some Church Fathers on music in the liturgy.[28] They saw Christian worship as the result of a process of "spiritualization" from the Temple cult of the Old Covenant with its animal sacrifices toward the *logikē latreia* (Rom 12:1), "worship in harmony with the eternal Word and with our rea-

---

The Advent Project: The Later-Seventh-Century Creation of the Roman Mass Proper (Berkeley, Los Angeles, and London: University of California Press, 2000), 19–98.

[27] See Ratzinger, "Artistic Transposition of the Faith", 490, with further references to D. Schuberth, *Kaiserliche Liturgie: Die Einbeziehung von Musikinstrumenten, insbesondere der Orgel, in den frühmittelalterlichen Gottesdienst*, Veröffentlichungen der Evangelischen Gesellschaft für Liturgieforschung 17 (Göttingen: Vandenhoeck & Ruprecht, 1968); E. Jammers, *Musik in Byzanz, im päpstlichen Rom und im Frankenreich: Der Choral als Textaussprache* (Heidelberg: C. Winter, 1962); E. Wellesz, *A History of Byzantine Music and Hymnography*, 2nd ed., revised and enlarged (Oxford: Clarendon Press, 1961).

[28] Ratzinger, "Artistic Transposition of the Faith", 487; cf. the collection of texts in McKinnon, *Music in Early Christian Literature*.

son".[29] If music was to prove adequate for the Christian liturgy, it also had to undergo a process of "spiritualization", which could be interpreted as a "de-materialization": music was admitted only insofar as it served the movement from the sensible to the spiritual; hence the discontinuity with the festive music of the Temple and the ban on instruments. However, there is an inherent ambiguity in the early Christians' austere attitude toward music, which Ratzinger attributes to the influence of Platonic thought on patristic theology. The consequence of this attitude, "which more or less borders on iconoclasm", is theology's "historical mortgage in the question of ecclesiastical art, which comes up over and over again".[30] The burden of this "mortgage" can be seen, for instance, in Saint Thomas Aquinas' treatment of sacred music in the *Summa Theologiae*.[31]

The development of Gregorian chant achieved a remarkable harmony between theological demands and the natural desire for artistic expression. However, the question of what distinguishes sacred music was bound to arise with the full development of polyphony starting in the twelfth century. In the thirteenth century, the problem arose that secular texts, such as love poetry, were inserted into church music, both in Latin and in the vernacular.

The move of the papacy to Avignon in 1309 brought a confrontation between the traditional Roman musical practice of plainchant and the French *ars nova*, which was

[29] A key theme in the thought of Benedict XVI; see *Faith, Reason and the University: Memories and Reflections: Lecture in the Aula Magna of the University of Regensburg* (September 12, 2006); see also *Sacramentum Caritatis*, no. 70, as well as *Spirit of the Liturgy*, 45–50 (JRCW 11:27–30).

[30] Ratzinger, "Artistic Transposition of the Faith", 488.

[31] Thomas Aquinas, *Summa Theologiae* II-II, q. 91, a. 2; Ratzinger discusses the patristic and philosophical background to Aquinas' treatment of sacred music in "On the Theological Basis of Church Music", 424–39.

introduced to the papal court. Pope John XXII addressed the question in his decree *Docta Sanctorum Patrum* of 1324/1325.[32] While he did not give general permission for polyphony, he stated that he did not intend

> to forbid the occasional use—principally on solemn feasts at Mass and in the Divine Office—of certain consonant intervals superposed upon the simple ecclesiastical chant, provided these harmonies are in the spirit and character of the melodies themselves, as, for instance, the consonance of the octave, the fifth, the fourth, and others of this nature: but always on condition that the melodies themselves remain intact in the pure integrity of their form and that no innovation take place against true musical discipline, for such consonances are pleasing to the ear and arouse devotion, and they prevent torpor among those who sing in honor of God.[33]

John XXII gave clear priority to plainchant and stipulated that in sacred music the formal structure of the chant be preserved both in its tonality (modes) and in its particular rhythmic movement. What makes plainchant eminently suitable to the liturgy is its sober character, and this can be perceived clearly in comparison with more elaborate and autonomous forms of polyphony, which do not meet with full approval in the papal document.[34] Although this is not made explicit in *Docta Sanctorum Patrum*, it would seem right

[32] Cf. R. F. Hayburn, *Papal Legislation on Sacred Music: 95 a.d. to 1977 a.d.* (Collegeville, Minn.: Liturgical Press, 1979; reprinted Harrison, N.Y.: Roman Catholic Books, 2006), 21. For a critical analysis of the decree, see H. Hucke, "Das Dekret 'Docta Sanctorum Patrum' Papst Johannes' XXII.", *Musica Disciplina* 38 (1984): 119–31.

[33] Trans. Hayburn, *Papal Legislation on Sacred Music*, 21, slightly modified.

[34] See K. G. Fellerer, "Die Constitutio Docta SS. Patrum Johannes XXII.", in *Geschichte der katholischen Kirchenmusik*, vol. 1: *Von den Anfängen bis zum Tridentinum*, ed. in K. G. Fellerer (Kassel: Bärenreiter, 1972), 379–80.

to conclude, as Joseph Ratzinger does, that a primary concern is the music's relation to the text, which is exemplary in plainchant; for this reason, the decree makes "reference to the formal structures of chant as the point of departure for ecclesiastical polyphony".[35]

The problem of defining criteria for sacred music presented itself more acutely with the development of Renaissance culture, and hence the question was discussed at the Council of Trent, although not before its final period between 1559 and 1563. Two main issues that had occupied local synods and individual bishops long before Trent emerged in the Council's deliberations: first, the integrity and intelligibility of the text set to music (which was also a general concern of musical humanists in the sixteenth century) and, secondly, the use of music from secular contexts in divine worship.[36]

In the twenty-second session of the Council in 1562, a committee drafted a canon that treated these aspects in a general way:

> Everything should indeed be regulated so that the Masses, whether they be celebrated with the plain voice or in song, with everything clearly and quickly executed, may reach the ears of the hearers and quietly penetrate their hearts. In those Masses where measured music and organ are customary, nothing profane should be intermingled, but only hymns and divine praises. . . . But the entire manner of singing in musical modes should be calculated, not to afford vain delight to the ear, but so that the words may be comprehensible to all; and thus may the hearts of the

[35] Ratzinger, "Artistic Transposition of the Faith", 492.

[36] Cf. C.A. Monson, "The Council of Trent Revisited", *Journal of the American Musicological Society* 55 (2002): 1–37, and, for the text of the most essential sources, Hayburn, *Papal Legislation on Sacred Music*, 25–31.

> listeners be caught up into the desire for celestial harmonies and contemplation of the joys of the blessed.[37]

However, this text was not included in the final *Decree concerning the Things to Be Observed, and to Be Avoided, in the Celebration of Mass*, which was promulgated on September 17, 1562. The decree contains only this very short paragraph on the matter:

> Let them keep away from the churches compositions in which there is an intermingling of the lascivious or impure, whether by instrument or voice.[38]

Thus only the question of the proper distinction between sacred and secular music entered the Council's decree, but not the central argument of the original draft on the intelligibility of the text sung at Mass, with its theological emphasis on the priority of the word.

The matter of sacred music was taken up again in the Council's twenty-fourth session in 1563, where a new impetus for Church reform was provided by the new papal legates, Cardinals Giovanni Morone and Bernardo Navagero, and by the papal confidant and later Cardinal Gabriele Paleotti. It was at this session that an attempt was made to ban polyphony from the sacred liturgy, as some prelates, among them Morone as Bishop of Modena, had already attempted

[37] In the English translation of Monson, "The Council of Trent Revisited", 9. For the Latin text, see: *Concilium Tridentinum: Diariorum, actorum, epistularum, tractatuum nova collectio*, ed. Societas Goerresiana (Freiburg: Herder, 1901–), 8:927. Ratzinger, "Artistic Transposition of the Faith", 492, quotes from this draft canon as if it were an official conciliar decree. This misreading is widespread and has even entered standard works of musicology, as noted by Monson, "Council of Trent Revisited", 11–12.

[38] Council of Trent, session 22, *Decree concerning the Things to Be Observed, and to Be Avoided, in the Celebration of Mass: Concilium Tridentinum*, 8: 963; English translation in Monson, "Council of Trent Revisited", 11.

to do in the first half of the sixteenth century.[39] Among those who strongly opposed such a proposal were Cardinal Otto Truchseß von Waldburg, Bishop of Augsburg,[40] and even Emperor Ferdinand I, who was alerted to the debate at the Council and intervened with a letter in August 1563.[41]

Historical scholarship has refuted the story that polyphony was saved when Pope Marcellus II, who reigned for less than a month in 1555, heard Palestrina's *Missa Papae Marcelli*, because, in fact, Palestrina had no influence on the debates about musical reform at the Council.[42] As for the *Missa Papae Marcelli*, it is more probable to see in it a creative response to the Council's reforming idea on sacred music.[43] Joseph Ratzinger has an interesting suggestion in this regard: the story that the immediate impact of hearing Palestrina's music averted a ban of polyphonic music in the liturgy expresses the truth that "the *composition* must be convincing, and not the theory, which can only follow the composition."[44]

[39] Cf. Monson, "Council of Trent Revisited", 13–14.

[40] C. T. Leitmeir and B. Klingenstein, "Catholic Music in the Diocese of Augsburg c. 1600: A Reconstructed Tricinium Anthology and Its Confessional Implications", *Early Music History* 21 (2002): 117–73, at 121–22.

[41] Cf. Monson, "Council of Trent Revisited", 13–14.

[42] The composer who can claim to have had some bearing on Trent's deliberations was the Franco-Flemish Jacobus de Kerle, whose *Preces speciales*, a set of polyphonic devotional responsories, were sung several times a week at prayer services during the last sessions of the Council. The musical setting was commissioned by Cardinal Otto Truchseß von Waldburg. See P. Bergin Jr., "*Preces Speciales:* Prototype of Tridentine Musical Reform", *The Ohio State Online Musical Journal* 2 (2009), http://osomjournal.org/issues/2/bergin/ (accessed March 26, 2015), with ample bibliography. The idea of Palestrina as the "savior" of sacred polyphony seems to have been presented first by the Sienese composer and music theorist Agostino Agazzari in 1607 and was then often repeated.

[43] This was suggested by K. G. Fellerer and M. Hadas, "Church Music and the Council of Trent", *The Musical Quarterly* 39 (1953): 576–94.

[44] Ratzinger, "Artistic Transposition of the Faith", 493.

In the end, the only pronouncement on the matter was included in the *Decree on Reform*, which delegates decisions on the Divine Office, including "the proper manner of singing or playing therein", to provincial synods. In the interim period before such synods are held, the local bishop, with the help of at least two canons, may provide as seems expedient.[45]

The question came up once again in the twenty-fifth session, when the practice of music in female religious houses was discussed and an attempt was made to exclude polyphony from convents altogether. However, there was opposition to this move, and in the end it was agreed that decisions on music should be made by the competent religious superiors.[46]

In sum, the Council said as little as possible on sacred music, but its discussion of it gave a strong impulse to local synods and bishops who implemented the Council's program for the reform of ecclesiastical life and discipline. In the years after Trent, the concerns for the intelligibility of the text and for an exclusion of secular music from the liturgy were perceived as being "secundum formam concilii". The practical solutions to these problems differed considerably from one place to the other, and this is reflected in the rich variety of polyphonic music at the time.[47]

The most important papal document on sacred music of the post-Tridentine period is Benedict XIV's encyclical letter *Annus Qui* of February 19, 1749. Its author, born Pros-

[45] Council of Trent, session 22, *Decree on Reform*, chap. 12: *Concilium Tridentinum*, 9:983–84.

[46] Cf. Monson, "Council of Trent Revisited", 19–22.

[47] Cf. ibid., 24; see also L. H. Lockwood, "Vincenzo Ruffo and Musical Reform after the Council of Trent", *The Musical Quarterly* 43 (1957): 342–71.

pero Lorenzo Lambertini, was a canonist and scholar with a wide range of interests; the actions and documents of his pontificate reflect a general concern for the Church's divine worship that includes theological, pastoral, and juridical aspects.[48] Under Benedict XIV, new editions of official liturgical books were published, among them the *Martyrologium Romanum* in 1748, the *Caeremoniale Episcoporum* in 1752, as well as various liturgical books of the Eastern Catholic Churches, to which the pope paid special attention. In 1740, he founded the now dormant Pontifical Academy for Liturgy. His liturgical Magisterium can be placed within the continuing project of reform championed by the Council of Trent. Some of the learned pope's theological and liturgical accents also show his attention to pastoral care and have a modern ring to them: he underlined the priority of observing the Sunday instead of the celebration of saints; he encouraged greater participation of the faithful in the celebration of the liturgy; he promoted more attention to Sacred Scripture in the liturgy; he also endorsed a historical methodology in the study of liturgical texts. At the same time, Benedict XIV's approach to the liturgy was conservative in the best sense, in that he sought to purify the sacred rites in the spirit of the Church's perennial tradition.[49]

The encyclical on sacred music, written for the Jubilee Year of 1750,[50] offers a number of criteria for sacred music

[48] His Brief *Sollicitudini Nostrae* of 1745 on questions of sacred art has been mentioned in chapter 4.

[49] See J. Hermans, *Benedictus XIV en de liturgie: Een bijdrage tot de liturgiegeschiedenis van de Moderne Tijd* (Brugge and Boxtel: Uitgeverij Emmaüs and Katholieke Bijbelstichting, 1979), 197–226.

[50] Both the Italian original and the Latin translation are available in *Sanctissimi domini nostri Benedicti Papae XIV: Bullarium, Tomus III* (Mechelen: Typis P.-J. Hanicq, 1827), 7:34–91; an English translation can be found in Hayburn, *Papal Legislation on Sacred Music*, 92–108.

that remain valid beyond the confines of their historical context and resonate in our time as well: it presents plainchant as normative for the Roman liturgy, while it also approves of unaccompanied polyphony and allows for orchestral music as long as it is distinct from the style of contemporary operas and cantatas. When the practice of orchestral music has already been introduced, it may continue, "as long as it is serious and does not, because of its length, cause boredom or serious inconvenience to those who are in choir, or who are celebrating at the altar, during Vespers and Mass".[51] In continuity with the discussions at the Council of Trent and the subsequent pronouncements of popes and local councils, the main concerns of Benedict XIV with regard to sacred polyphony are the integrity and the intelligibility of the liturgical texts of the Mass and the Divine Office. The encyclical *Annus Qui* in many ways anticipates Saint Pius X's better-known Motu Proprio *Tra le Sollecitudini* of 1903; however, its reach was limited, and it had little effect outside the Papal States, where Benedict XIV was able to implement its norms directly.

[51] Translation Hayburn, *Papal Legislation on Sacred Music*, 104. Sources from the archives of Benedict XIV help to illustrate the background of this statement: a memorandum of Roman origin notes that the length of a musical piece should correspond to the length of the liturgical action and not unnecessarily prolong it. The older Roman school of polyphony is presented as a model, because its Mass compositions correspond in length to the time it takes the celebrant to perform the respective ritual action. Andrea Adami, master of the papal choir from 1700 to 1714, writes in his notes about the practice of the Sistine Chapel that particular attention was paid to the coordination between the musicians and the celebrant with his assistance. By contrast, a description of a Mass in Germany of 1784 observes that the celebrant had to wait several times until the music finished in order to continue with the liturgical action. See C. Bacciagaluppi, "'E viva Benedetto XIV!' L'enciclica *Annus qui* (1749) nel contesto dei rapporti musicali tra Roma e Bologna", in *Papsttum und Kirchenmusik vom Mittelalter bis zu Benedikt XVI.: Positionen—Entwicklungen—Kontexte*, ed. K. Pietschmann, Analecta musicologica 47 (Kassel: Bärenreiter, 2012), 222–62.

Church music being unduly influenced by popular culture is not just a phenomenon of the later twentieth century. The novel *La Regenta* (The judge's wife) by the Spanish writer Leopoldo Alas (also known under his pseudonym Clarín), published in 1884 and 1885, provides a somewhat humorous insight into the practice of church music at the time. The realistic novel, set in the provincial capital "Vetusta" (which can be identified with Oviedo, where Alas spent most of his life), includes the description of a Christmas Midnight Mass: "To express the Christian joy of this sublime moment the organ was recalling traditional tunes of the region and songs which popular caprice had made fashionable during recent years." The narrator comments: "There were no barriers in that place, at that moment, between the church and the world." Among the ephemeral tunes the organ played were those "of joyful fiestas in the country, of sailors' songs by the side of the sea". After the Epistle, which introduced a more serious note, the organist gave "faulty renderings of the toast from *La Traviata* and the Miserere from *Il Trovatore*". This culminated, just before the Gospel, in an otherwise unknown song called "La Mandilona", with the text: "So now you're just as glad as you could, wish, / Jellyfish, / Jellyfish, / Jellyfish"—which was greeted with "whispers and stifled laughter".[52]

An echo of similar musical malpractice is found in Giuseppe Tomasi di Lampedusa's historical novel *Il Gattopardo* (*The Leopard*), published posthumously in 1958. After arriving in their summer retreat at Donnafugata (the scene is set in August 1860), the Prince of Salina with his family enters the church for the *Te Deum*; the organist, Don Ciccio Tumeo, breaks "impetuously into the strains of Verdi's

[52] L. Alas, *La Regenta*, trans. J. Rutherford, Penguin Classics (London: Penguin, 1984, reprinted with corrections 2005), vol. 2, XXIII, 530 and 531. I gratefully owe the reference to this work to Martin Mosebach.

Amami, Alfredo" from *La Traviata.*[53] The scene is well captured in Luchino Visconti's masterful film adaption of 1963.

Even when we make allowance for literary embellishment, it is against this backdrop that we should understand the sober judgment on the state of church music given by Pope Saint Pius X in his Motu Proprio *Tra le Sollecitudini* of November 22, 1903. The pontiff singles out for criticism "the theatrical style that was so much in vogue during the last century," as the one least fitted for liturgical worship.[54]

Tra le Sollecitudini became a foundational document for liturgical renewal in the twentieth century; its main objective is the restoration of sacred music, and to this end it formulates general principles in continuity with previous magisterial pronouncements:

> Sacred music, being a complementary part of the solemn liturgy, participates in the general scope of the liturgy, which is the glory of God and the sanctification and edification of the faithful. It contributes to the decorum and the splendor of the ecclesiastical ceremonies, and since its principal office is to clothe with suitable melody the liturgical text proposed for the understanding of the faithful, its proper aim is to add greater efficacy to the text, in order that through it the faithful may be the more easily moved to devotion and better disposed for the reception of the fruits of grace belonging to the celebration of the most holy mysteries.[55]

[53] G. Tomasi di Lampedusa, *The Leopard*, trans. A. Colquhoun, rev. ed. (London: Vintage, 2007), 44.

[54] Pope Pius X, Motu Proprio *Tra le Sollecitudini* on the Restoration of Sacred Music (November 22, 1903), Instruction on Sacred Music, II. The different kinds of sacred music, 6. English version quoted from http://adoremus.org/MotuProprio.html. The Motu Proprio, originally written in Italian, had already been prepared by Cardinal Giuseppe Sarto as a pastoral letter for his Diocese of Venice and was issued only months after his election to the See of Peter.

[55] Pius X, *Tra le Sollecitudini*, Instruction on Sacred Music, I. General Principles, 1.

While the Motu Proprio's emphasis on the priority of the liturgical text resumes a primary objective of the Tridentine reform, its understanding of the ministerial role of sacred music in the Church's worship looks forward to *Sacrosanctum Concilium*. Perhaps the most notable contribution of *Tra le Sollecitudini* consists in the three criteria it proposes for sacred music:

> Sacred music should consequently possess, in the highest degree, the qualities proper to the liturgy, and in particular sanctity and goodness of form, which will spontaneously produce the final quality of universality.[56]

The first criterion, "sanctity (*la santità*)", is thoroughly traditional and restates the Church's concern with a proper distinction of sacred from secular use, which became acute with the development of polyphony in the later Middle Ages. The second criterion, "goodness of form (*la bontà delle forme*)" (later in the document also invoked as "true art [*arte vera*]"), is remarkable because it recognizes man's natural desire for artistic expression more explicitly than any previous document on church music. The insistence on certain quality standards also calls for the corresponding technical skills of composition and execution. According to the mind of Pius X, when these two criteria are met, the third one, universality, will follow of itself. The demand for universality can provide a corrective, where needed, for particular cultural forms, but it does not suppress them:

> [Sacred music] must, at the same time, be universal in the sense that while every nation is permitted to admit into its ecclesiastical compositions those special forms which may be said to constitute its native music, still these forms must be subordinated in such a manner to the general character-

[56] Ibid., General Principles, 2.

istics of sacred music that nobody of any nation may receive an impression other than good on hearing them.[57]

In continuity with ecclesiastical tradition, the Motu Proprio extols Gregorian chant, "the Chant proper to the Roman Church", and recommends classical polyphony, above all the Roman school shaped by Palestrina. At the same time, more recent and contemporary forms of music are encouraged, if they meet the criteria presented for sacred music.[58] *Tra le Sollecitudini* was a formative influence on *Sacrosanctum Concilium*'s chapter on sacred music (see above), and its principles have been restated by subsequent popes.[59]

Benedict XVI and Sacred Music

Having at some length discussed the contributions Joseph Ratzinger made as a theologian to questions of sacred music, it will be instructive to take account of the pronouncements he made as pope on the subject. There are several relevant passages in his first Post-Synodal Apostolic Exhortation *Sacramentum Caritatis* of 2007. In continuity with *Sacrosanctum Concilium*, the importance of the assembly's singing "the praises of God" in the liturgy is highlighted, and, at the same time, the Church's tradition of sacred music is affirmed as "a rich patrimony of faith and love", which "must not be lost". Of particular note is the statement that, "as far as the liturgy is concerned, we cannot say that one song is as good as another." In other words, there are definite criteria that music

[57] Ibid., 2.

[58] Cf. ibid., 3–5.

[59] Paul VI, *Address to the Participants in the General Assembly of the Italian Association Santa Cecilia* (September 18, 1968); John Paul II, *Chirograph for the Centenary of the Motu Proprio "Tra le Sollecitudini" on Sacred Music* (November 22, 2003); Benedict XVI, *Address at the Visit to the Pontifical Institute for Sacred Music* (October 13, 2007).

needs to observe if it is to be introduced into the liturgy. The apostolic exhortation specifies that "everything—texts, music, execution—ought to correspond to the meaning of the mystery being celebrated, the structure of the rite and the liturgical seasons." While allowing for a variety of styles and traditions, Gregorian chant is once again recommended and exalted as "the chant proper to the Roman liturgy".[60] There is one reason above all why Gregorian chant is so eminently suitable for the liturgy: its innate relationship to the biblical text, to which it gives musical form, as Benedict XVI explains in his second Post-Synodal Apostolic Exhortation *Verbum Domini* of 2010.[61] In *Sacramentum Caritatis*, the pope asks that candidates for the priesthood, "from their time in the seminary", should "receive the preparation needed to understand and to celebrate Mass in Latin, and also to use Latin texts and execute Gregorian chant". The faithful on their part should be able "to sing parts of the liturgy to Gregorian chant".[62]

The Motu Proprio *Summorum Pontificum* of 2007 is of special importance for church music.[63] The Extraordinary Form, or *usus antiquior*, of the Roman Rite is intimately

[60] Benedict XVI, *Sacramentum Caritatis*, no. 42.

[61] Benedict XVI, Post-Synodical Apostolic Exhortation *Verbum Domini* on the Word of God in the Life and Mission of the Church (September 30, 2010), no. 70: "As part of the enhancement of the word of God in the liturgy, attention should also be paid to the use of song at the times called for by the particular rite. Preference should be given to songs which are of clear biblical inspiration and which express, through the harmony of music and words, the beauty of God's word. We would do well to make the most of those songs handed down to us by the Church's tradition which respect this criterion. I think in particular of the importance of Gregorian chant."

[62] Benedict XVI, *Sacramentum Caritatis*, no. 62.

[63] Benedict XVI, Apostolic Letter given Motu Proprio *Summorum Pontificum* (July 7, 2007); see also Pontifical Commission *Ecclesia Dei*, Instruction *Universae Ecclesiae* on the Application of the Apostolic Letter *Summorum Pontificum* given Motu Proprio (April 30, 2011).

connected with Gregorian chant, because its sung forms, the *Missa cantata* and Solemn High Mass, require the chanting of the Mass Propers, whereas in the Ordinary Form these can be replaced by other "apt" or "congruous" forms of music, the texts of which are approved by the local conference of bishops, as is granted by the *General Instruction of the Roman Missal.*[64] Moreover, it is impressive to experience the great works of sacred polyphony in the ritual setting for which they were actually composed. For these reasons, *Summorum Pontificum* is a strong signal to foster and promote traditional church music.[65]

In this regard, mention should be made of Pope Benedict's own liturgical celebrations. As he said in December 2005 to the members of the Sistine Chapel Choir, the "Pope's liturgy, the liturgy in St. Peter's, must be an example of liturgy for the world". Thanks to the electronic media, today people all over the world are able to follow the liturgical celebrations of the Supreme Pontiff. "From here", he adds, "they learn or do not learn what the liturgy is, how the liturgy should be celebrated." Therefore, the Sistine Choir has a particular responsibility to set an example "of how to convey beauty in song, in praise of God".[66]

In the first years of his pontificate, the liturgical celebrations of Benedict XVI did not show a particular profile, as

[64] *Missale Romanum ex decreto Sacrosancti Oecumenici Concilii Vaticani II instauratum auctoritate Pauli PP. VI promulgatum Ioannis Pauli PP. II cura recognitum.* Editio typica tertia, reimpressio emendata (Vatican City: Typis Vaticanis, 2008), *Institutio Generalis Missalis Romani*, nos. 48 and 87.

[65] Cf. G. P. Weishaupt, *Päpstliche Weichenstellungen: Das Motu Proprio* Summorum Pontificum *Papst Benedikts XVI. und der Begleitbrief an die Bischöfe: Ein kirchenrechtlicher Kommentar und Überlegungen zu einer "Reform der Reform"* (Bonn: Verl. für Kultur und Wissenschaft, 2010), 132–38.

[66] Benedict XVI, *Address to the Members of the Pontifical "Sistine" Choir* (December 20, 2005).

far as sacred music was concerned. This changed with the appointment of the Salesian Father Massimo Palombella as director of the Sistine Chapel Choir in October 2010 in replacement of Msgr. Giuseppe Liberto, who had held this office since 1997. Among the changes that were introduced by Palombella at papal masses, there was, for instance, the singing of *Tu es Petrus* in the setting of Palestrina or Lorenzo Perosi, when the pope entered Saint Peter's Basilica in procession. Notably, most of the Mass Propers were sung in Gregorian chant according to the *Graduale Romanum*. There was a manifest desire to recover the traditions of Roman sacred music under the given conditions in Italy, which are not favorable at all to such an enterprise because of the low standards of musical culture in general and in particular in the ecclesiastical sphere. It would seem that this particular aspect of Benedict's liturgical celebrations is continued and consolidated in the pontificate of Francis.

Practical Considerations

As a conclusion to this chapter, I should like to make three suggestions regarding the practice of sacred music today. The first one relates to the introduction of new forms of music into the liturgy with the good intention of giving it a more festive character. This phenomenon is a reaction to the banalization of sacred music in the postconciliar years and can be observed at great events, such as World Youth Days and Eucharistic Congresses. Such music, however, often has a sentimental character and requires orchestras with all kinds of instruments, which in the Latin tradition (to say nothing here of the Eastern churches) were discouraged or even considered unsuitable. It is also in striking contrast to the simplicity and sobriety of the Gregorian settings of the Ordinary of the Mass. At this point one may ask why sentimentality should not have a place in divine worship. A lucid response to this question is given by the American literary writer Flannery O'Connor, who considers sentimentality "an excess, a distortion of sentiment, usually in the direction of an overemphasis on innocence".[67] O'Connor is concerned here with the writing of fiction, in particular with the problems faced by a professedly Catholic author, but her reflections are pertinent to our discussion as well. Sentimentality is an attempted shortcut to lost innocence that ignores the price that had to be paid for our redemption of the world:

> We lost our innocence in the fall of our first parents, and our return to it is through the redemption which was brought about by Christ's death and by our slow participation in it. Sentimentality is a skipping of this process in its concrete reality and an early arrival at a mock state of innocence, which strongly suggests its opposite.[68]

A timely antidote against the spiritual sentimentality of much present musical practice can be found in the earlier Christian tradition with its insistence on sobriety in liturgical music. At the same time, one needs to avoid the "iconoclastic" tendencies of this tradition, which may be owing

[67] F. O'Connor, "The Church and the Fiction Writer", *America*, March 30, 1957, available on http://americamagazine.org/issue/100/church-and-fiction-writer (accessed March 24, 2014).

[68] For O'Connor, the opposite of sentimentality in literature is the obscene. She regards pornography as "essentially sentimental, for it leaves out the connection of sex with its hard purposes, disconnects it from its meaning in life and makes it simply an experience for its own sake": ibid. Cf. R. C. Wood, "Christian Skepticism vs. Religious Sentimentality", chap. 7 of *Contending for the Faith: The Church's Engagement with Culture* (Waco, Tex.: Baylor University Press, 2003), 123–34.

to the influence of Platonism on patristic thought, as has been discussed. In the Roman liturgy, this is achieved in an exemplary way by Gregorian chant.

There is another point to consider in this regard: the music promoted at mass events is theatrical and usually excludes the "active participation" of the faithful. We would do much better to acquaint the faithful over the course of time with several plainchant Masses (not just the *De Angelis*) that could then be sung together by the participants in large international gatherings. Gregorian chant is a unique treasure we have received from our ancestors in the faith, and it immediately appeals to people's sense of the sacred even in our age. Why else would it be played through loudspeakers in historical cathedrals and churches that are much visited by tourists during the day if not to remind them that they are in a sacred space? Gregorian chant also addresses the question of inculturation because it transcends the boundaries of particular cultures and therefore has a universal appeal. It is happily sung by Catholics in Africa and Asia, just as in Europe or North America. Let me refer here to the enlightening observation of the German literary author Martin Mosebach:

> This music had sounded strange even to the ears of Charlemagne and Thomas Aquinas, Monteverdi and Haydn: it was at least as remote from their contemporary life as it is from ours—for we find it much easier to tune in to the music of other cultures than people of earlier times did.[69]

Secondly and consequent upon the first observation, the use of instruments in the liturgy needs to be carefully reviewed. The Christian tradition is consistent in giving

[69] M. Mosebach, *The Heresy of Formlessness: The Roman Liturgy and Its Enemy*, trans. G. Harrison (San Francisco: Ignatius Press, 2006), 16.

priority to the human voice in divine worship. The Latin West has not been as strict as the Eastern rites in excluding the use of instruments. The organ has enjoyed a special place in the Western liturgy ever since its introduction in the eighth or ninth century. At first sight, the reasons for this development do not seem evident: the organ was played as part of Roman imperial ceremonial, a practice that continued in Byzantium (in the palace and in the hippodrome), but it did not have a liturgical function. When the organ became known in the Frankish realm, through the donation of an instrument to the Carolingian court, it was adapted for liturgical use, in a process that cannot be retraced sufficiently owing to a lack of sources. Initially, it would seem to have been used to sustain plainchant and later polyphony.[70] As an autonomous form of music that would accompany certain moments in liturgical celebrations, organ playing developed slowly and gradually. Ever since, as William P. Mahrt notes, the very use of the large pipe organ singles it out as a sacred instrument:

> It is not regularly heard anywhere but in church. Musical instruments have the property of being able to remind us of the location of the usual performance, just like incense and chant. The sound of the organ recalls the locus of the church. The piano recalls, at best, the home or the concert hall, or worse, the cocktail lounge or daytime television, depending partly upon the style of music played on it.[71]

[70] Cf. Wellesz, *History of Byzantine Music and Hymnography*, 105–9, and Schuberth, *Kaiserliche Liturgie*, 114–34.

[71] W. P. Mahrt, "Music and the Sacrality of the Two Forms", in *Benedict XVI and the Roman Missal: Proceedings of the Fourth Fota International Liturgical Conference, 2011*, ed. J. E. Rutherford and J. O'Brien, Fota Liturgy Series (Dublin and New York: Four Courts Press and Scepter Publishers, 2013), 192–207, at 197.

Recognizing the organ as a church instrument in this sense obviously involves a process of reception that could theoretically be reversed, even though this convention is still firmly rooted in Western consciousness. There is, however, another more profound characteristic that makes the organ innately suitable for its sacred purpose, and that is its similarity to the human voice:

> The tone of the organ is sustained, like the singing of the voice, while the tone of the piano has a percussive beginning and an immediate decay, very unvocal. I believe it has been a serious mistake to introduce the piano into regular use in church. Needless to say, this applies to the guitar even more.[72]

It is therefore not simply an accident of history that the organ was introduced into Western liturgy, let alone that it *remained* there through the centuries and in various cultural contexts, despite the persistent reservations about the use of instruments in church (which are still present in Benedict XIV's *Annus Qui*, as seen above). Even today, the organ should have pride of place, while other instruments should be used with discretion and sobriety. At the same time, the organ should be in the service of the liturgy; while there is room for artistic expression, especially before a celebration and at its very end, its playing should not be autonomous in the same way as in a recital or concert.

My third suggestion concerns the widespread replacement of the Proper chants of the Roman Mass with other "apt" or "congruous" forms of music, as permitted by the *General Instruction of the Roman Missal.*[73] Naturally it requires

[72] Ibid.

[73] *Institutio Generalis Missalis Romani*, nos. 48 and 87. Unlike the *Graduale*

a considerable effort to put together a schola capable of singing the chants from the *Graduale Romanum*, and so, in practice, all kinds of music, more or less "apt", are substituted for it. This music is often of low quality, influenced by pop culture, and is hardly appropriate for the sacred liturgy. Part of the problem is that until recently no clear norms were given to regulate new forms of liturgical music. This issue has been resolved to some extent by the Instruction *Liturgiam Authenticam* of 2001, which stipulates that "the Conferences of Bishops . . . shall provide for the publication of a directory or repertory of texts intended for liturgical singing." Such a directory is to be submitted to the Congregation for Divine Worship and the Discipline of the Sacraments for the *recognitio* of the Holy See.[74]

However, even where these criteria are fulfilled or where a traditional repertory of high-quality hymns exists, such as in England or Germany, the consequence is still that, despite the constant teaching of the Church, Gregorian chant is, *de facto*, no longer the proper music of the Roman liturgy. This is not just a musical loss; it also affects the integrity of the liturgical texts. The disappearance of the Gregorian Propers "means that the Church today no longer speaks through the chants of the Mass: that the chants effectively have no part at all in forming the liturgy and delivering its message", as Laszlo Dobszay put it. The intimate connection between liturgy and music is severed.[75]

Romanum, the Missal does not consider what is sung during the Offertory part of the liturgical text, cf. no. 74.

[74] Congregation for Divine Worship and the Discipline of the Sacraments, Fifth Instruction for the Right Implementation of the Constitution on the Sacred Liturgy of the Second Vatican Council *Liturgiam Authenticam* (March 28, 2001), no. 108.

[75] L. Dobszay, "The *Proprium Missae* of the Roman Rite", in *The Genius*

This also affects the proper celebration of liturgical times and seasons. There is a tendency in parishes and communities today to sing the same repertory of music from Sunday to Sunday, a tendency that obscures the rhythm and flow of the liturgical year. Advent is a case in point: it is a time of expectation, of waiting, indeed, of longing for the coming of the Savior, the desired One of all nations. It is a time of holy joy; this can be sensed in the chants of the Mass and the antiphons of the Divine Office for the Sundays of Advent. However, this joy is interior rather than exterior, and Advent also has an atmosphere of sobriety, including penitential elements. Violet vestments are used, the altars are rather bare, the *Gloria* is not sung at Sunday Mass, and the organ should be silent apart from accompanying the singing. All too often, however, the general influence of consumerist society affects the celebration of the liturgy, so that Christmas is unduly anticipated, while Advent loses its proper character. Music has an important role in shaping the liturgical year, and the Gregorian chant repertory is exemplary in this regard.

---

of the Roman Liturgy: Historical Diversity and Spiritual Reach: Proceedings of the 2006 Oxford CIEL Colloquium, ed. U. M. Lang (Chicago: Hillenbrand Books, 2010), 83–118, at 93–94. *Liturgiam Authenticam*, no. 60, confronts this serious matter: "Whether it be a question of the texts of Sacred Scripture or of those taken from the Liturgy and already duly confirmed, paraphrases are not to be substituted with the intention of making them more easily set to music, nor may hymns considered generically equivalent be employed in their place." However, the reference to *Institutio Generalis Missalis Romani*, nos. 53 and 57, at the end of this paragraph would seem to limit the scope of this prescription, because no. 53 refers only to the *Gloria* at Mass and no. 57 prohibits the substitution of scriptural text in the Liturgy of the Word. See also W. P. Mahrt, "The Propers of the Mass as Integral to the Liturgy", in *Benedict XVI and Beauty in Sacred Music: Proceedings of the Third Fota International Liturgical Conference, 2010*, ed. J. E. Rutherford, Liturgy Series (Dublin and New York: Four Courts Press and Scepter Publishers, 2012), 149–62.

The implementation of the new *Roman Missal* in the English-speaking world has provided a unique opportunity to address this problem, and the recent diffusion of resources, for instance, by Adam Bartlett and Richard Rice, for singing the Ordinary and the Propers of the Mass in plainchant melodies based on the Gregorian modes is a promising development.[76] Such resources are essential to bridge the gap that exists between the centers of musical excellence and the ordinary parish with its limited capacities. Promoting simplified forms of singing the Mass (and not just singing something during Mass, to paraphrase a dictum attributed to Saint Pius X), whether in Latin or in the vernacular, is a key element of promoting authentic liturgical piety.

Sacred music cannot, of course, be limited to plainchant, and it is enriched by more recent musical forms, including those coming from the Russian Orthodox, Anglican, and Lutheran traditions. However, I am convinced that Gregorian chant holds the key for a true renewal of church music today.

[76] See A. Bartlett, *Simple English Propers: For the Ordinary Form of Mass, Sundays and Feasts* (Richmond, Va.: CMAA, 2011); R. Rice, *Simple Choral Gradual: Settings for Mixed Choir of the Entrance, Offertory, and Communion Antiphons for Sundays and Solemnities of the Church Year* (Richmond, Va.: CMAA, 2011).

EPILOGUE

Ongoing Liturgical Renewal and the Problem of Ritual Change

The question of ritual change has been touched upon in the first chapter of this book. Ritual as a system of symbolic communication is characterized by custom, rigor, and repetition. Hence it gives the impression of being perennial, and it is precisely this stability that makes it work as ritual. Whether or not such claims are made explicitly, rites embody the traditions of the community formed by them. Ritual change is a problem *per se*, because it conveys the message that there was something wrong with the previous ritual forms. It can even have a lasting detrimental effect on the system of symbolic communication as such, by suggesting that ritual does not matter in the end.

This delicate working of ritual was not sufficiently recognized in the liturgical reform following the Second Vatican Council, even where it was applied with the best intentions. Among the various reasons for this short-sightedness was the at least implicit assumption that established ritual forms could easily be exchanged and replaced with their historical antecedents. Martin Mosebach has commented lucidly on the dynamic of ritual change in an essay on kneeling, standing, and walking in the liturgy. The ancient and venerable posture of standing is a sign of awe in the presence of God as well as a proclamation of Christ's Resurrection and the worshipper's participation in it. This practice has been maintained as a living tradition in the Eastern Christian rites. In the West, however, kneeling has become the people's common expression of prayer and adoration, especially in the most sacred parts of the Mass. This was the fruit of an interplay between ever more fervent devotion to and doctrinal clarifications of the Eucharistic mystery in the Middle Ages. Kneeling in the presence of the Blessed Sacrament was promoted in particular by Saint Francis of Assisi and his movement as a part of lay piety.[1] This development has shaped Western consciousness, and, as a consequence, Mosebach notes, "standing has lost all significance as a specific gesture."[2] When therefore a deliberate effort was made in the postconciliar period to promote the posture of standing in those parts of the Mass when the people were used to kneeling, the result was a significant loss in symbolic communication, which also affected the understanding of the faith: "Whereas the early Christians, by standing at the liturgy, expressed the fact that they were celebrating a sacrificial meal, it often happens that contemporary worshippers stand to express the opposite—that they are *not* participating in a sacrifice. Kneeling speaks an unmistakable language; standing does not. Nowadays standing is felt to show less reverence than kneeling."[3]

The postconciliar liturgical reform, by virtue of having been "the most extensive renewal of the Roman Rite ever known" (Benedict XVI),[4] has highlighted the dilemma of

[1] Cf. A. Thompson, *Francis of Assisi: A New Biography* (Ithaca, N.Y.: Cornell University Press, 2012), 83–84.

[2] M. Mosebach, *The Heresy of Formlessness: The Roman Liturgy and Its Enemy*, trans. G. Harrison (San Francisco: Ignatius Press, 2006), 124.

[3] Ibid., 133. On the use of the body in ritual see also R. A. Rappaport, *Ritual and Religion in the Making of Humanity*, Cambridge Studies in Social and Cultural Anthropology (Cambridge: Cambridge University Press, 1999), 146.

[4] Benedict XVI, *Video Message for the Closing of the 50th International Eucharistic Congress in Dublin* (June 17, 2012).

ritual change. Whatever the merits of its particular elements, the rapid and often abrupt implementation of the reform has dramatically accelerated a process already under way in the Western Church that can be described as an alienation from the ritual expression of the sacred. Much has been written in recent years on particular problems, which at some distance from the actual reform can now be seen more clearly. What most critics of the present situation identify can be subsumed under three headings: first, external activism and the loss of mystery, rooted in a horizontal, self-contained notion of the liturgy that does not transcend ordinary experience; secondly, a restriction of the Holy Eucharist to its moment of celebration and an artificial contrast, if not conflict, with its dimension of adoration;[5] thirdly, liturgical "creativity" and anomy, which suggest that the liturgy is a space devoid of laws. This last phenomenon goes beyond the often-addressed question of "liturgical abuses", that is, infringement of existing liturgical legislation. A mentality of lawlessness is a consequence of the alienation from ritual, which was engendered by the tremendous speed with which the liturgy was changed. Moreover, ambiguous elements in the postconciliar liturgical books have contributed to ritual instability, above all, the options for adapting rites to given circumstances and the frequent *ad libitum* passages ("with these or similar words"). Although they do of course not explicitly condone it, they convey the impression that liturgical rules can easily be bent and need not be strictly observed.

In this situation, Benedict XVI has called for an effort to resume the liturgical renewal desired by the Second Vatican Council in a different key.[6] It is my conviction that

[5] Benedict XVI, *Homily for the Solemnity of Corpus Christi* (June 7, 2012).

[6] Benedict XVI, *Video Message for the Closing of the 50th International Eucharistic Congress in Dublin* (June 17, 2012).

this would above all require the acknowledgment that infelicitous decisions have been made in the implementation of the Council's principles for a renewal of divine worship and that too little consideration has been given the general norm of *Sacrosanctum Concilium*, no. 23, that "there must be no innovations unless the good of the Church genuinely and certainly requires them; and care must be taken that any new forms adopted should in some way grow organically from forms already existing."

In concrete terms, this would mean reconsidering the process of liturgical renewal according to the hermeneutic of reform in continuity in interpreting the Council. However, the manifest discontinuity in the ritual practice of the Church has created a situation in which a mere imposition of traditional liturgical forms would be widely perceived as yet another rupture. This dilemma was keenly felt by Pope Benedict XVI, who as a theologian reflected extensively on the subject. For this reason he chose another approach in his Motu Proprio *Summorum Pontificum* by lifting previous restrictions on the use of the preconciliar liturgical books and making them the "Extraordinary Form" or *usus antiquior* of the *one* Roman Rite. This decision is not without its conceptual and practical difficulties, because there are profound differences between the two forms in the prayers and readings, the structure of the liturgical year, and in many particular ritual elements of the Mass (leaving aside here the other sacraments, which raise similar questions). From the ritual perspective, the two forms converge, when, for instance, the postconciliar Mass is celebrated in Latin and at an altar facing east instead of facing the people and when the faithful are encouraged to kneel for the reception of Holy Communion. While the differences remain, the characteristic spirit or *ethos* informing the ritual expression of the sacred is essentially the same.

Hence to speak of two forms of the same rite would seem to describe the intended goal of a process that was meant to begin with *Summorum Pontificum.* This was to be achieved through the "mutual enrichment" of the two forms in an "organic" way that would avoid the discontinuity that did so much damage to Catholic ritual in the postconciliar period. It would seem to have been the idea of Benedict XVI that this should happen as if by osmosis, that is, a steady and, as it were, unconscious assimilation of the liturgical tradition. An important element in this process was to be the pontiff's example in his own celebrations. Ritual elements such as the placing of a prominent crucifix in the center of the altar, the distribution of Holy Communion to the faithful kneeling and directly on the tongue, and the extended use of the Latin language were intended to set a standard to be imitated. However, since the liturgy is the public and ordered worship of the Church, such a process needs to be sustained by liturgical legislation, at least in the form of opening possibilities and providing encouragement, as happened in the case of *Summorum Pontificum.* The fact that this did not happen in the pontificate of Benedict XVI was not only a lost opportunity but also suggested that these measures were simply expressions of a pope's personal preferences that can easily be reversed by his successors. Nonetheless, perspectives for a renewal in continuity with the liturgical tradition have been opened and are taken up especially by younger generations in the Church throughout the world. This "new liturgical movement" has the potential to mend the torn threads of Catholic ritual, but this is a work that will need patience and perseverance and will not be completed in our lifetime.

Bibliography

Ancient, medieval and early modern sources, which are quoted in the individual chapters of the book according to their current critical editions, are not included in this bibliography. The texts of papal and curial documents are taken from the Vatican website (www.vatican.va) unless otherwise noted.

Alas, L. *La Regenta*. Translated by J. Rutherford. Penguin Classics. London: Penguin, 1984. Reprinted with corrections, 2005.

Ansideri. *La Bottega dell'Architetto: Conversazione con Massimiliano Fuksas sulla chiesa di Foligno . . . ed altro*. Rome, April 17, 2009. http://oicosriflessioni.it/wp-content/uploads/2011/07/corretto-Paolo-05-10-11-intervista-fuksas.pdf.

Archer, A. *The Two Catholic Churches: A Study in Oppression*. London: SCM Press, 1986.

Audet, J.-P. "Le sacré e le profane: leur situation en christianisme". *Nouvelle Revue théologique* 79 (1957): 33–61.

Bacciagaluppi, C. "'E viva Benedetto XIV!' L'enciclica *Annus qui* (1749) nel contesto dei rapporti musicali tra Roma e Bologna". In *Papsttum und Kirchenmusik vom Mittelalter bis zu Benedikt XVI.: Positionen—Entwicklungen—Kontexte*, edited by K. Pietschmann, 222–62. Analecta musicologica 47. Kassel: Bärenreiter, 2012.

Baldovin, J. F. *The Urban Character of Christian Worship: The Origins, Development, and Meaning of Stational Liturgy*. Orientalia Cristiana Analecta 228. Rome: Pont. Institutum Studiorum Orientalium, 1987. Anastatic reproduction, 2002.

Bartlett, A. *Simple English Propers: For the Ordinary Form of Mass, Sundays and Feasts*. Richmond, Va.: CMAA, 2011.

Baumgärtel-Fleischmann, R. *Die Altäre des Bamberger Domes von 1012 bis zur Gegenwart*. With the collaboration of B. Neundorfer, B. Schemmel, W. Milutzki. Veröffentlichungen des Diözesan-Museums Bamberg 4. Bamberg: Bayerische Verlagsanstalt, 1987.

Becker, T. A. "The Role of *Solemnitas* in the Liturgy according to Saint Thomas Aquinas". In *Rediscovering Aquinas and the Sacraments: Studies in Sacramental Theology*, edited by M. Levering and M. Dauphinais, 114–35. Chicago: Hillenbrand, 2009.

Bell, C. *Ritual: Perspectives and Dimensions*. New York: Oxford University Press, 1997.

———. *Ritual Theory, Ritual Practice*. New York: Oxford University Press, 1992. Reprinted, 2009.

Benedict XIV. Encyclical Letter *Annus Qui* (February 19, 1749). In *Sanctissimi domini nostri Benedicti Papae XIV. Bullarium, Tomus III*, 7:34–91. Mechelen: Typis P.-J. Hanicq, 1827.

Benedict XVI. *Address at Heiligenkreuz Abbey* (September 9, 2007).

———. *Address at the Meeting with Artists in the Sistine Chapel* (November 21, 2009).

———. *Address at the Visit to the Pontifical Institute for Sacred Music* (October 13, 2007).

———. *Address to the Members of the Pontifical "Sistine" Choir* (December 20, 2005).

———. Apostolic Letter given Motu Proprio *Summorum Pontificum* (July 7, 2007).

———. *Christmas Address to the Members of the Roman Curia* (December 22, 2005).

———. *Faith, Reason and the University: Memories and Reflection: Lecture in the Aula Magna of the University of Regensburg* (September 12, 2006).

———. *Homily at the Holy Mass for the Solemnity of Corpus Christi* (June 7, 2012).

———. *Homily at the Mass of Possession of the Chair of the Bishop of Rome* (May 7, 2005).

———. *Homily for the Chrism Mass* (April 9, 2009).

———. *Meeting with the Clergy of the Diocese of Bolzano-Bressanone* (August 6, 2008).

———. *Message for the Centenary of the Birth of Fr Hans Urs von Balthasar* (October 6, 2005).

———. *Message on the Occasion of the 13th Public Conference of the Pontifical Academies* (November 24, 2008).

———. "On the Inaugural Volume of My Collected Works". In J. Ratzinger, *Theology of the Liturgy: The Sacramental Foundation of Christian Existence*, xv–xviii. Vol. 11 of *Joseph Ratzinger Collected Works*. San Francisco: Ignatius Press, 2014.

———. Post-Synodal Apostolic Exhortation *Sacramentum Caritatis* on the Eucharist as the Source and Summit of the Church's Life and Mission (February 22, 2007).

———. Post-Synodal Apostolic Exhortation *Verbum Domini* on the Word of God in the Life and Mission of the Church (September 30, 2010).

———. *Video Message at the Closing Mass of the 50th International Eucharistic Congress* (June 17, 2012).

Benedict XVI. *See also* Ratzinger, J.

Benjamin, W. "Das Kunstwerk im Zeitalter seiner technischen Reproduzierbarkeit (Dritte Fassung)". In *Gesammelte Schriften*, vol. 1, *Werkausgabe*, vol. 2, edited by R. Tiedemann and H. Schweppenhäuser, 471–508. Frankfurt am Main: Suhrkamp, 1980.

Bergin, Jr., P. "*Preces Speciales:* Prototype of Tridentine Musical Reform". *The Ohio State Online Musical Journal* 2 (2009). http://osomjournal.org/issues/2/bergin.html.

Bodei, R. *Le forme del bello*. Bologna: Il Mulino, 1995.

Boespflug, F. *Dieu dans l'art: "Sollicitudini Nostrae" de Benoît XIV (1745) e l'affaire Crescence de Kaufbeuren*. Paris: Cerf, 1984.

Bossy, J. *Christianity in the West, 1400–1700*. Oxford: Oxford University Press, 1985.

Botta, M. "Lo spazio del sacro". In *Architetture del sacro: Preghiere di pietra*, ed. G. Cappellato, 3–5. Bologna: Editrice Compositori, 2005.

———. "Räume des Übergangs". In M. Botta, G. Böhm, P. Böhm, R. Moneo. *Sakralität und Aura in der Architektur*, 10–51. Architekturvorträge der ETH Zürich. Zürich: GTA Verlag, 2010.

Bouyer, L. *Rite and Man: The Sense of the Sacral and Christian Liturgy*. Translated by M. J. Costelloe. London: Burns & Oates, 1963.

———. "Two Temptations". *Worship* 37 (1962): 11–21.

Bühren, R. van. "Kirchenbau in Renaissance und Barock: Liturgiereformen und ihre Folgen für Raumordnung, liturgische Disposition und Bildausstattung nach dem Trienter Konzil". In *Operation am lebenden Objekt: Roms Liturgiereformen von Trient bis zum Vaticanum II*, edited by S. Heid, 93–119. Berlin: be.bra wissenschaft, 2014.

———. *Kunst und Kirche im 20. Jahrhundert: Die Rezeption des Zweiten Vatikanischen Konzils*. Paderborn: Schöningh, 2008.

Bultmann, R. *Das Evangelium des Johannes*. Meyers kritisch-exegetischer Kommentar über das Neue Testament 2. 21st ed. Göttingen: Vandenhoeck & Ruprecht, 1986.

Burke, P. *Reinterpreting Rahner: A Critical Study of His Major Themes*. New York: Fordham University Press, 2002.

Catechism of the Catholic Church. 2nd ed. Vatican City and Washington, D.C.: Libreria Editrice Vaticana, 2000.

Cattaneo, E. *Arte e liturgia dalle origini al Vaticano II*. Milan: Vita e pensiero, 1982.

Chenis, C. *Fondamenti teorici dell'arte sacra: Magistero post-conciliare*. Rome: Libreria Ateneo Salesiano, 1991.

Clair, J. *Considérations sur l'état des beaux-arts: Critique de la modernité*. Paris: Gallimard, 1983.

———. "Culte de l'avant-garde e culture de mort". http://chiesa.espresso.repubblica.it/articolo/1348110?fr=y (extracts in English: http://chiesa.espresso.repubblica.it/articolo/13 48149?eng=y).

Compendium: Catechism of the Catholic Church. Washington, D.C.: United States Conference of Catholic Bishops, 2006.

Concilium Tridentinum: Diariorum, actorum, epistularum, tractatuum nova collectio. Edited by Societas Goerresiana. Freiburg: Herder, 1901–.

Congregation for Divine Worship and the Discipline of the Sacraments. Fifth Instruction for the Right Implementation of the Constitution on the Sacred Liturgy of the Second Vatican Council *Liturgiam Authenticam* (March 28, 2001).

———. Instruction *Redemptionis Sacramentum* on Certain Matters to Be Observed or to Be Avoided regarding the Most Holy Eucharist (March 25, 2004).

Csikszentmihalyi, M. *Beyond Boredom and Anxiety.* San Francisco: Jossey-Bass, 1975.

Denzinger, H. *Enchiridion Symbolorum: Compendium of Creeds, Definitions, and Declarations of the Catholic Church.* Edited by P. Hünermann, H. Hoping, R. Fastiggi, and A. Englund Nash. 43rd ed. San Francisco: Ignatius Press, 2012.

Deshusses, J. *Le sacramentaire grégorien: Ses principales formes d'après les plus anciens manuscrits*, vol. 1. Spicilegium Friburgense 16. 3rd ed. Fribourg: Éditions Universitaires, 1992.

Dobszay, L. "The *Proprium Missae* of the Roman Rite". In *The Genius of the Roman Liturgy: Historical Diversity and Spiritual Reach: Proceedings of the 2006 Oxford CIEL Colloquium*, ed. U.M. Lang, 83–118. Chicago: Hillenbrand Books, 2010.

Doig, A. *Liturgy and Architecture: From the Early Church to the Middle Ages.* Liturgy, Worship and Society. Farnham and Burlington, Vt.: Ashgate, 2008.

Dole, A. "Schleiermacher and Otto on Religion". *Religious Studies* 40 (2004): 389–413.

Donati, C. "A colloquio con Mario Botta: le nuove forme della memoria". *Costruire in Laterizio* 72 (November/December 1999): 40–44.

Doorly, M. *No Place for God: The Denial of the Transcendent in Modern Church Architecture*. San Francisco: Ignatius Press, 2007.

Douglas, M. *Natural Symbols: Explorations in Cosmology*. 2nd ed. London and New York: Routledge, 1996.

Droste, B. *"Celebrare" in der römischen Liturgiesprache*. Munich: Hueber, 1963.

Durkheim, É. *The Elementary Forms of the Religious Life*. Translated by J. W. Swain. London: Allen & Unwin, 1915.

Eliade, M. *The Sacred and the Profane: The Nature of Religion*. Translated by W. R. Trask. New York: Harcourt, Brace, 1959.

Fellerer, K. G. "Die Constitutio Docta SS. Patrum Johannes XXII.". In *Geschichte der katholischen Kirchenmusik*, vol. 1, *Von den Anfängen bis zum Tridentinum*, edited by K. G. Fellerer, 379–80. Kassel: Bärenreiter, 1972.

———, and M. Hadas. "Church Music and the Council of Trent". *The Musical Quarterly* 39 (1953): 576–94.

Feuillet, A. *Le sacerdoce du Christ et de ses ministres d'après la prière sacerdotale du quatrième Évangile et plusieurs données parallèles du Nouveau Testament*. Paris: Téqui, 1997.

Gagliardi, M. *Liturgia fonte di vita*. Verona: Fede & Cultura, 2009.

Gatti, V. *Liturgia e arte: I luoghi della celebrazione*. Bologna: EDB, 2001.

Geertz, C. "Religion as a Cultural System". In *The Interpretation of Cultures: Selected Essays*, 87–125. New York: Basic Books, 1973.

Geldhof, J. "The Early and Late Schillebeeckx OP on Rituals, Liturgies, and Sacraments". *Usus Antiquior* 1 (2010): 132–50.

Gilley, S. "Newman, Pugin and the Architecture of the English Oratory". In *Modern Christianity and Cultural Aspirations*, edited by D. Bebbington and T. Larsen, 98–123. London and New York: Sheffield Academic Press, 2003.

———. "Roman Liturgy and Popular Piety: The 'Devotional Revolution' in Irish Catholicism". In *The Genius of the Roman Rite: Historical, Theological and Pastoral Perspectives on Catholic Liturgy: Proceedings of the 2006 Oxford CIEL Colloquium*, edited by U. M. Lang, 216–34. Chicago: Hillenbrand Books, 2010.

Hauke, M. "Karl Rahner nella critica di Leo Scheffczyk". In *Karl Rahner: Un'analisi critica: La figura, l'opera e la recezione teologica di Karl Rahner (1904–1984)*, edited by S. M. Lanzetta, 267–87. Siena: Cantagalli, 2009.

Hayburn, R. F. *Papal Legislation on Sacred Music: 95 a.d. to 1977 a.d.* Collegeville, Minn.: Liturgical Press, 1979. Reprinted, Harrison, N.Y.: Roman Catholic Books, 2006.

Heathcote, E., and I. Spens. *Church Builders*. Chichester: Academy Editions, 1997.

Hecht, C. *Katholische Bildertheologie im Zeitalter von Gegenreformation und Barock: Studien zu Traktaten von Johannes Molanus, Gabriele Paleotti und anderen Autoren*. 2nd revised and enlarged ed. Berlin: Gebr. Mann, 2012.

Hermans, J. *Benedictus XIV en de liturgie: Een bijdrage tot de liturgiegeschiedenis van de Moderne Tijd*. Brugge and Boxtel: Uitgeverij Emmaüs and Katholieke Bijbelstichting, 1979.

Hitchcock, J. *The Recovery of the Sacred*. New York: Seabury Press, 1974.

Hucke, H. "Das Dekret 'Docta Sanctorum Patrum' Papst Johannes' XXII.". *Musica Disciplina* 38 (1984): 119–31.

Jammers, E. *Musik in Byzanz, im päpstlichen Rom und im Frankenreich: Der Choral als Textaussprache*. Heidelberg: C. Winter, 1962.

John Paul II. *Address to the Bishops of the Episcopal Conference of the United States of America (Washington, Oregon, Idaho, Montana and Alaska)* (October 9, 1998).

———. *Chirograph for the Centenary of the Motu Proprio "Tra le Sollecitudini" on Sacred Music* (November 22, 2003).

Kavanagh, A. *On Liturgical Theology: The Hale Memorial Lectures of Seabury-Western Theological Seminary, 1981*. Collegeville, Minn.: Liturgical Press, 1984.

Kermani, N. *Gott ist schön: Das ästhetische Erleben des Koran*. Munich: C. H. Beck, 1999.

Kimball, R. "The End of Art". *First Things* 184 (June/July 2008): 27–31.

———. "The Vocation of Art". In *Religion and the American Future*, edited by C. DeMuth and Y. Levin, 179–207. Washington, D.C.: AEI Press, 2008.

Laing, A. "Baroque Sculpture in a Neo-Baroque Setting". In *The London Oratory: Centenary 1884–1984*, edited by M. Napier and A. Laing, 56–83. London: Trefoil, 1984.

Lang, U. M. "Tamquam Cor in Pectore: The Eucharistic Tabernacle before and after the Council of Trent". *Sacred Architecture Journal* 15 (2009): 32–34.

———. *Turning Towards the Lord: Orientation in Liturgical Prayer*. 2nd ed. San Francisco: Ignatius Press, 2009.

———. *The Voice of the Church at Prayer: Reflections on Liturgy and Language*. San Francisco: Ignatius Press, 2012.

Le Corbusier. *Œuvre complète*. Vol. 5, *1946–52*. Edited by W. Boesiger. Basel: Birkhäuser, 2006.

Leitmeir, C. T., and B. Klingenstein. "Catholic Music in the Diocese of Augsburg c. 1600: A Reconstructed Tricinium Anthology and Its Confessional Implications". *Early Music History* 21 (2002): 117–73.

Lévi-Strauss, C. *Structural Anthropology*. Translated by C. Jacobson and B. Grundfest Schoepf. New York: Basic Books, 1963.

Lockwood, L. H. "Vincenzo Ruffo and Musical Reform after the Council of Trent". *The Musical Quarterly* 43 (1957): 342–71.

Lynch, G. *On the Sacred*. Durham: Acumen, 2012.

Mahrt, W. P. "Commentary on *Sing to the Lord*". In *The Musical Shape of the Liturgy*, 165–78. Richmond, Va.: Church Music Association of America, 2012.

———. "Music and the Sacrality of the Two Forms". In *Benedict XVI and the Roman Missal: Proceedings of the Fourth Fota International Liturgical Conference, 2011*, edited by J. E. Rutherford and J. O'Brien, 192–207. Fota Liturgy Series. Dublin and New York: Four Courts Press and Scepter Publishers, 2013.

———. "The Paradigm: The Musical Shape of the Liturgy, Part I: The Gregorian Mass in General". In *The Musical Shape of the Liturgy*, 3–16. Richmond, Va.: Church Music Association of America, 2012.

———. "The Propers of the Mass as Integral to the Liturgy". In *Benedict XVI and Beauty in Sacred Music: Proceedings of the Third Fota International Liturgical Conference, 2010*, edited by J. E. Rutherford, 149–62. Fota Liturgy Series. Dublin and New York: Four Courts Press and Scepter Publishers, 2012.

McDonald, M. "Creative Restoration". *Traditional Building* 25 (2012): 28–31.

McKinnon, J. *The Advent Project: The Later-Seventh-Century Creation of the Roman Mass Proper*. Berkeley, Los Angeles, and London: University of California Press, 2000.

———. *Music in Early Christian Literature*. Cambridge Readings in the Literature of Music. Cambridge: Cambridge University Press, 1987. Reprinted 1993.

McNamara, D. R. "A Decade of New Classicism: The Flowering of Traditional Church Architecture". *Sacred Architecture* 21 (2012): 18–24.

———. *How to Read Churches: A Crash Course in Ecclesiastical Architecture*. New York and Lewes: Rizzoli, 2011.

Missale Romanum ex decreto Sacrosancti Oecumenici Concilii Vaticani II instauratum auctoritate Pauli PP. VI promulgatum. Editio typica. Vatican City: Typis Polyglottis Vaticanis, 1970.

Missale Romanum ex decreto Sacrosancti Oecumenici Concilii Vaticani II instauratum auctoritate Pauli PP. VI promulgatum Ioannis Pauli PP. II cura recognitum. Editio typica tertia, reimpressio emendata. Vatican City: Typis Vaticanis, 2008.

Missale Romanum ex decreto SS. Concilii Tridentini restitutum Summorum Pontificum cura recognitum. Editio typica. Vatican City: Typis Polyglottis Vaticanis, 1962.

Moneo, R. "Cathedral of Our Lady of the Angels Los Angeles, CA, 1996–2002". In *Sakralität und Aura in der Architektur* by M. Botta, G. Böhm, P. Böhm, and R. Moneo, 84–105. Architekturvorträge der ETH Zürich. Zürich: GTA Verlag, 2010.

Monson, C. A. "The Council of Trent Revisited". *Journal of the American Musicological Society* 55 (2002): 1–37.

Mosebach, M. *Du sollst dir ein Bild machen: Über alte und neue Meister*. Springe: zu Klampen, 2005.

———. *The Heresy of Formlessness: The Roman Liturgy and Its Enemy*. Translated by G. Harrison. San Francisco: Ignatius Press, 2006.

Murphy, F. A. *Christ the Form of Beauty: A Study in Theology and Literature*. London: Continuum, 1995.

Muti, R. "Introduzione". In J. Ratzinger (Benedetto XVI), *Lodate Dio con arte: Sul canto e sulla musica*, edited by C. Carniato, 7–11. Venice: Marcianum Press, 2010.

Newman, J. H. "The Gospel Palaces". In *Parochial and Plain Sermons*, 1354–60. San Francisco: Ignatius Press, 1997.

———. *The Letters and Diaries of John Henry Newman*. Vol. 12, *Rome to Birmingham January 1847 to December 1848*. Edited by C. S. Dessain. London: Nelson, 1962.

Nichols, A. *Looking at the Liturgy: A Critical View of Its Contemporary Form*. San Francisco: Ignatius Press, 1996.

O'Connor, F. "The Church and the Fiction Writer". *America* (March 30, 1957), http://americamagazine.org/issue/100/church-and-fiction-writer.

Ordo Missae in cantu iuxta editionem typicam tertiam Missalis Romani. Solesmes: Éd. de Solesmes, 2012.

Otto, R. *The Idea of the Holy: An Inquiry into the Non-Rational Factor in the Idea of the Divine and Its Relation to the Rational*. Translated by J. W. Harvey. Revised with additions. Oxford and London: Oxford University Press and Humphrey Milford, 1936.

Palazzo, E. "Art et liturgie au Moyen Âge: Nouvelles approches anthropologique et épistémologique". In *Anales de Historia del Arte*, Volumen extraordinario 2010: 31–74.

———. "Art, Liturgy and the Five Senses in the Early Middle Ages". *Viator* 41 (2010): 25–56.

———. "La dimension sonore de la liturgie dans l'Antiquité chrétienne et au Moyen Âge". In *Archéologie du son: Les dispositifs de pots acoustiques dans les édifices anciens*, edited by B. Palazzo-Bertholon and J.-C. Valière, 51–58. Supplément au Bulletin monumental 5. Paris: Société Française d'Archéologie, 2012.

Paleotti, G. *Discorso intorno alle immagini sacre e profane (1582)*. Edited by S. Della Torre. Vatican City: Libreria Editrice Vaticana, 2002.

Papa, R. "Riflessioni sui fondamenti dell'arte sacra". *Euntes docete* 3 (1999): 327–41.

Paul VI. *Address to the Participants in the General Assembly of the Italian Association Santa Cecilia* (September 18, 1968).

———. *Homily at the "Mass of the Artists" in the Sistine Chapel* (May 7, 1964).

———. *Message to Artists at the Closing of the Second Vatican Council* (December 8, 1965).

Pieper, J. *In Search of the Sacred.* Translated by L. Krauth. San Francisco: Ignatius Press, 1991.

———. "Sakralität und 'Entsakralisierung' (1969)". In *Werke*. Vol. 7, *Religionsphilosophische Schriften*, edited by B. Wald, 394–419. Hamburg: Felix Meiner, 2000.

———. "Zur Fernseh-Übertragung der Heiligen Messe (1953)". In *Werke*. Vol. 7, *Religionsphilosophische Schriften*, edited by B. Wald, 487–90. Hamburg: Felix Meiner, 2000.

Pius X. Motu Proprio *Tra le Sollecitudini* on the Restoration of Sacred Music (November 22, 1903). http://www.adoremus.org/MotuProprio.html.

Pius XII. *Discours aux fidèles, retransmis pour la première fois par la télévision française* (April 17, 1949).

———. Encyclical Letter on the Sacred Liturgy *Mediator Dei* (November 20, 1947).

Pontifical Commission *Ecclesia Dei*. Instruction *Universae Ecclesiae* on the Application of the Apostolic Letter *Summorum Pontificum* given Motu Proprio (April 30, 2011).

Proust, M. "La Mort des cathédrales". *Le Figaro*, August 16, 1904: 3.

Pugin, A. W. N. *The True Principles of Pointed or Christian Architecture.* London: John Neale, 1841. Reprinted with an introduction by R. O'Donnell. Leominster: Gracewing, 2003.

Rahner, K. "Considerations on the Active Role of the Person in the Sacramental Event". In *Theological Investigations.* Vol. 14, *Ecclesiology, Questions in the Church, the Church in the World*, translated by D. Bourke, 161–84. New York: Seabury Press, 1976.

———. "Kleine Vorüberlegung über die Sakramente im allgemeinen". In *Über die Sakramente der Kirche: Meditationen*, 11–21. Freiburg: Herder, 1985.

———. "Die Messe und das Fernsehen". *Orientierung* 17 (1953): 179–83.

———. "On the Theology of Worship". In *Theological Investigations*. Vol. 19, *Faith and Ministry*, translated by E. Quinn, 141–49. New York: Crossroad, 1983.

———. "Sakrament: V. Systematik". In *Lexikon für Theologie und Kirche*, 2nd ed., 9:227–30 (1964).

———, and H. Vorgrimler. *Kleines Konzilskompendium*. 2nd ed. Freiburg: Herder, 1967.

Rappaport, R. A. *Ecology, Meaning, and Religion*. Richmond, Calif.: North Atlantic Books, 1979.

———. *Ritual and Religion in the Making of Humanity*. Cambridge Studies in Social and Cultural Anthropology. Cambridge: Cambridge University Press, 1999.

Ratzinger, J. "The Artistic Transposition of the Faith: Theological Problems of Church Music". In JRCW 11:480–93.

———. "Catholicism After the Council". Translated by P. Russell. *The Furrow* 18 (1967): 3–23.

———. "The Image of the World and of Human Beings in the Liturgy and Its Expression in Church Music". In JRCW 11:443–60.

———. Introduction to *Compendium: Catechism of the Catholic Church*, 13–15. Washington, D.C.: United States Conference of Catholic Bishops, 2006.

———. (Benedict XVI). *Jesus von Nazareth*. Part 2, *Vom Einzug in Jerusalem bis zur Auferstehung*. Freiburg: Herder,

2011. Translated by P. J. Whitmore as *Jesus of Nazareth. Part 2, Holy Week: From the Entrance into Jerusalem to the Resurrection*. San Francisco: Ignatius Press, 2011.

———. *Milestones: Memoirs (1927–1977)*. Translated by Erasmo Leiva-Merikakis. San Francisco: Ignatius Press, 2005.

———. "On the Theological Basis of Church Music". In JRCW 11:421–42.

———. Preface to *The Organic Development of the Liturgy: The Principles of Liturgical Reform and Their Relation to the Twentieth-Century Liturgical Movement Prior to the Second Vatican Council*, by A. Reid, 9–13. 2nd ed. San Francisco: Ignatius Press, 2005. JRCW 11:589–94.

———. Preface to *Turning Towards the Lord: Orientation in Liturgical Prayer*, by U. M. Lang, 9–12. 2nd ed. San Francisco: Ignatius Press, 2009. JRCW 11:393–95.

———. *The Spirit of the Liturgy*. Translated by J. Saward. San Francisco: Ignatius Press, 2000. JRCW 11:1–150.

———. "Theology of the Liturgy: A Lecture Delivered during the Journées Liturgiques de Fontgombault, 22–24 July 2001". In JRCW 11:541–57.

———. *Theology of the Liturgy: The Sacramental Foundation of Christian Existence*. Edited by M. J. Miller. Translated by J. Saward, K. Baker, S.J., H. Taylor et al. Vol. 11 of *Joseph Ratzinger Collected Works*. San Francisco: Ignatius Press, 2014. JRCW 11.

———. "Wounded by the Arrow of Beauty: The Cross and the New 'Aesthetics' of Faith". In *On the Way to Jesus Christ*, translated by M. J. Miller, 32–41. San Francisco: Ignatius Press, 2005.

Ratzinger, J. *See also* Benedict XVI.

Reid, A. *The Organic Development of the Liturgy: The Principles of Liturgical Reform and Their Relation to the Twentieth-Century Liturgical Movement Prior to the Second Vatican Council*, 9–13. 2nd ed. San Francisco: Ignatius Press, 2005.

———. "Sacred Music and Actual Participation in the Liturgy". In *Benedict XVI and Beauty in Sacred Music: Proceedings of the Third Fota International Liturgical Conference, 2010*, edited by J. E. Rutherford, 93–126. Fota Liturgy Series. Dublin and New York: Four Courts Press and Scepter Publishers, 2012.

Rice, R. *Simple Choral Gradual: Settings for Mixed Choir of the Entrance, Offertory, and Communion Antiphons for Sundays and Solemnities of the Church Year*. Richmond, Va.: CMAA, 2011.

Ries, J. "*Homo religiosus*, sacré, sainteté". In *L'expression du sacré dans les grandes religions*. Vol. 3, *Mazdéisme, cultes isiaques, religion grecque, Manichéisme, Nouveau Testament, vie de l'Homo religiosus*, edited by J. Ries, 331–84. Homo religiosus 3. Louvain-la-Neuve: Centre d'Histoire des Religions, 1986.

Roman Missal: Renewed by Decree of the Most Holy Second Ecumenical Council of the Vatican, Promulgated by Authority of Pope Paul VI and Revised at the Direction of Pope John Paul II. English translation according to the third typical edition. London: Catholic Truth Society, 2011.

Rosen, D. *Verdi: Requiem*. Cambridge Music Handbooks. Cambridge: Cambridge University Press, 1995.

Sacred Congregation for the Sacraments and Divine Worship. Instruction *Inaestimabile Donum* concerning Worship of the Eucharistic Mystery (April 17, 1980).

Sardar, Z. "Cathedral Dreams". *San Francisco Chronicle Magazine* (February 18, 2001). http://www.sfgate.com/bayarea/article/CATHEDRAL-DREAMS-Celebrated-for-skeletal-2950579.php.

Schillebeeckx, E. *Christ the Sacrament of the Encounter with God*. New York: Sheed and Ward, 1963.

Schloeder, S. J. *Architecture in Communion: Implementing the Second Vatican Council through Liturgy and Architecture*. San Francisco: Ignatius Press, 1998.

Schuberth, D. *Kaiserliche Liturgie: Die Einbeziehung von Musikinstrumenten, insbesondere der Orgel, in den frühmittelalterlichen Gottesdienst*. Veröffentlichungen der Evangelischen Gesellschaft für Liturgieforschung 17. Göttingen: Vandenhoeck & Ruprecht, 1968.

Scruton, R. *Beauty*, Oxford: Oxford University Press, 2009.

Second Vatican Council. Constitution on the Sacred Liturgy *Sacrosanctum Concilium* (December 4, 1963).

———. Pastoral Constitution on the Church in the Modern World *Gaudium et Spes* (December 7, 1965).

Sekretariat der Deutschen Bischofskonferenz. *Gottesdienst-Übertragungen in Hörfunk und Fernsehen. Leitlinien und Empfehlungen 2002*. 2nd ed., 2007. dbk.de/fileadmin/redaktion/veroeffentlichungen/arbeitshilfen/AH_169.pdf.

Seligman, A. B., R. P. Weller, M. J. Puett, and B. Simon. *Ritual and Its Consequences: An Essay on the Limits of Sincerity*. New York: Oxford University Press, 2008.

Senn, F. C. *The People's Work: A Social History of the Liturgy*. Minneapolis: Fortress Press, 2006.

Seveso, B. "La trasmissione televisiva della messa nelle valutazioni del magistero ecclesiastico". *Rivista liturgica* 84 (1997): 89–109.

Skelley, M. *The Liturgy of the World: Karl Rahner's Theology of Worship*. Foreword by R. G. Weakland. Collegeville, Minn.: Liturgical Press, 1991.

Stosur, D. A. *The Theology of Liturgical Blessing in the Book of Blessings: A Phenomenologico-theological Investigation of a Liturgical Book*. Ph.D. dissertation. University of Notre Dame, 1994.

Stroik, D. G. "The Roots of Modernist Church Architecture". *Adoremus Bulletin* 3 (1997). Online edition, http://www.adoremus.org/1097-Stroik.html.

———. *The Church Building as a Sacred Place: Beauty, Transcendence, and the Eternal*. Chicago: Hillenbrand Books, 2012.

Tambiah, S. J. "A Performative Approach to Ritual". *Proceedings of the British Academy* 65 (1979): 113–69.

Thompson, A. *Francis of Assisi: A New Biography*. Ithaca, N.Y.: Cornell University Press, 2012.

Tomasi di Lampedusa, G. *The Leopard*. Translated by A. Colquhoun. Revised ed. London: Vintage, 2007.

Torevell, D. *Losing the Sacred: Ritual, Modernity and Liturgical Reform*. Edinburgh: T&T Clark, 2000.

Turner, V. "Frame, Flow and Reflection: Ritual and Drama as Public Liminality". *Japanese Journal of Religious Studies* 6 (1979): 465–99.

———. "Passages, Margins, and Poverty: Religious Symbols of Communitas". *Worship* 46 (1972): 390–412 and 482–94.

———. *The Ritual Process: Structure and Anti-Structure*. With a foreword by R. D. Abrahams. Piscataway, N.J.: Aldine Transaction, 1969. Second printing, 2008.

———. "Ritual, Tribal and Catholic". *Worship* 50 (1976): 504–26.

———, and E. Turner. *Image and Pilgrimage in Christian Culture: Anthropological Perspectives*. New York: Columbia University Press, 1978.

United States Conference of Catholic Bishops. *Guidelines for Televising the Liturgy*. 2014. www.usccb.org/prayer-and-worship/liturgical-resources/the-mass/frequently-asked-questions/guidelines-for-televising-the-liturgy.cfm.

———. *Sing to the Lord: Music in Divine Worship*. Washington, D.C.: USCCB Publishing, 2008.

Van Gennep, A. *The Rites of Passage*. Translated by M. B. Vizedom and G. L. Caffee. Chicago: University of Chicago Press, 1960.

Verdon, T. "Anche il Beato Angelico era un astrattista". *L'Osservatore Romano*, January 12, 2008: 5.

Viladesau, R. *Theological Aesthetics: God in Imagination, Beauty, and Art*. Oxford and New York: Oxford University Press, 1999.

Von Balthasar, H. U. *The Glory of the Lord*. Vol. 1, *Seeing the Form*. Translated by E. Leiva-Merikakis. San Francisco: Ignatius Press, 1982.

Watkin, D. *Morality and Architecture: The Development of a Theme in Architectural History and Theory from the Gothic Revival to the Modern Movement*. Oxford: Clarendon Press, 1977.

Weakland, R. "Music as Art in Liturgy". *Worship* 41 (1967): 5–15.

Weishaupt, G. P. *Päpstliche Weichenstellungen: Das Motu Proprio* Summorum Pontificum *Papst Benedikts XVI. und der Begleitbrief an die Bischöfe. Ein kirchenrechtlicher Kommentar und Überlegungen zu einer "Reform der Reform"*. Bonn: Verl. für Kultur und Wissenschaft, 2010.

Wellesz, E. *A History of Byzantine Music and Hymnography*. 2nd ed., revised and enlarged. Oxford: Clarendon Press, 1961.

Wood, R. C. *Contending for the Faith: The Church's Engagement with Culture*. Waco, Tex.: Baylor University Press, 2003.

Zecchi, S. *L'artista armato: Contro i crimini della modernità*. Milan: Mondadori, 1998.

Zumstein, J. *L'Évangile selon saint Jean (13–21)*. Commentaire du Nouveau Testament. Second series, IVb. Geneva: Labor et Fides, 2007.